Miracle Evangelism

By John Ezekiel

ISBN 0-941975-38-X

© Copyright 1991, 1995

It is illegal and a violation of Christian ethics to reproduce any part of this manual without the written permission of the author.

*Powerhouse Publishing
P.O. Box 99
Fawnskin, CA 92333
(909) 866-3119*

Manuals in This Series

Authority of the Believer
*How to Quit Losing and
Start Winning*

The Church Triumphant
Through the Book of Acts

God's Provision for Healing
*Receiving and Ministering
God's Healing Power*

Ministry Gifts
*Apostle, Prophet, Evangelist,
Pastor, Teacher*

New Creation Image
Knowing Who You Are in Christ

Patterns for Living
From the Old Testament

Praise and Worship
Becoming Worshipers of God

Supernatural Living
*Through the Gifts of the
Holy Spirit*

Miracle Evangelism

Foreword By A.L. Gill

When God spoke about publishing a manual on miracle evangelism, our thoughts went immediately to John Ezekiel of Johor Bahru, Malaysia. We met him on our first trip to Malaysia in 1984 and we have never known a person more consumed with the desire to reach souls for Jesus. Person to person, leading a group from his church, or conducting huge evangelistic meetings, his calling is the same – that of the evangelist.

Since meeting him, we have ministered together throughout West and East Malaysia, India, Pakistan, Mauritius, Andaman Islands, Finland, Korea and in the United States. Together, we have seen the book of Acts come alive with thousands coming to Jesus as God continues to confirm His word with signs, wonders, and healing miracles. John's ministry is touching people from every ethnic and religious background as they witness the awesome demonstrations of the healing power of God.

What John has written, he has proved in his own life. This is not a collection of theories, but has been written from a lifetime of learning and doing the works of evangelism. As you study this manual, you will thrill at biblical examples of miracle evangelism in action in the daily encounters of personal evangelism and before multitudes.

From the examples of evangelism in the ministry of Jesus, the disciples, and the early believers like Peter, John, Philip and Paul, we learn evangelism was always accompanied by miracles. There is no biblical pattern for evangelism apart from miracle evangelism.

In our lifetime, God has been restoring miracles to mass evangelism. Now, He is restoring miracles to the daily witness of believers. In the Great Commission, Jesus made it clear that signs were to follow those who believe as they preached the gospel. His parting words continue to compel us into action today: "They will lay hands on the sick, and they will recover."

Challenged, commissioned and empowered like the early believers, we will experience the joy of the Lord working with us as we proclaim His gospel. "And they went out and preached everywhere, the Lord working with them and confirming the word through the accompanying signs."

When Peter and John ministered healing to the crippled man laying at the gate called Beautiful, a crowd gathered. Peter preached about Jesus, the Source of that miracle, and five thousand men heard the message and believed.

Philip went to Samaria and when the crowds heard Philip and saw the miraculous signs he did, they paid close attention to what he said. With shrieks, evil spirits came out. Many paralytics and cripples were healed. So there was great joy in that city. The account continues, "When the apostles in Jerusalem heard that Samaria had accepted the word of God ..." It appears that the whole town accepted Jesus!

Paul wrote, "My speech and my preaching were not with persuasive words of human wisdom, but in demonstration of the Spirit and power." Paul's preaching and teaching in Ephesus was accompanied by miracles. "Now God worked unusual miracles by the hands of Paul, so that even handkerchiefs or aprons were brought from his body to the sick, and the diseases left them and the evil spirits went out of them."

The key to reaching the world with the gospel, whether our next door neighbor or going to the ends of earth, is found in this powerful study. It's miracle evangelism restored to the hands of every believer.

A Word to Teachers and Students

Miracle Evangelism is a powerful study which will release believers into becoming daily soul winners in the great end-time harvest through miracle evangelism. Like the believers in the book of Acts, we can experience the joy of reaching the lost as God confirms His word through signs, wonders and healing miracles.

We suggest that before teaching this course, you saturate yourself with the truths of God's word concerning evangelism and the Great Commission. We suggest that you "stir up within you" and "fan into flame" the power gifts of the Holy Spirit, so that God will continually confirm His word through signs and wonders. This manual will then provide the outline for you to use as you impart these truths to others so that they too will experience the joy of miracle evangelism in their daily lives.

Personal life illustrations are a must for effective teaching. The author has omitted these from this work so that the teacher will provide illustrations from his or her own rich experiences, or those of others to which the students will be able to relate.

It should always be remembered that it's the Holy Spirit who has come to teach us all things, and that when we are studying or when we are teaching we should always be empowered and led by the Holy Spirit.

This study is excellent for personal or group studies, Bible schools, Sunday schools and home groups. It's important that both the teacher and the student have copies of this manual during the course of the study.

The best books are written in, underlined, meditated on and digested. We have left space for your notes and comments. The format has been designed with a fast reference system for review and to assist you in finding areas again. The special format makes it possible for each person, once they have studied through this material, to teach the contents to others.

Paul wrote to Timothy: **And the things you have heard me say in the presence of many witnesses entrust to reliable men who will also be qualified to teach others. 2 Timothy 2:2b**

This course is designed as a practical participation Bible course in the MINDS (Ministry Development System) format which is a specially developed approach to programmed learning. This concept is designed for multiplication in the lives, the ministry and the future teaching of the students. Former students, by using this manual, can teach this course easily to others.

Contents

Lesson 1	The Great Commission	7
Lesson 2	Revival for Our Time!	15
Lesson 3	The Church Triumphant	23
Lesson 4	Authority of the Believer	31
Lesson 5	Militant Evangelism	39
Lesson 6	Releasing the Global Harvest	47
Lesson 7	The Army of God	53
Lesson 8	Power Evangelism in Action	61
Lesson 9	Ministering by the Anointing	69
Lesson 10	The Gifts of the Spirit	79
Lesson 11	Ministering Healing and Deliverance	91
Lesson 12	Finances and the Pioneer Spirit	99

*The Scriptures used in **Miracle Evangelism**
are from the **New King James Version of the Bible**.
Copyright 1979 by Thomas Nelson Inc.,
Publishers, Nashville, Tennessee, U.S.A.*

Lesson One

The Great Commission

Jesus gave His last instructions just before He left the earth. These words are referred to as the Great Commission.

The Great Commission is not just a suggestion or a request. It's a command from the King of kings and the Lord of lords! Jesus said we are to bring the total ministry of Jesus to the uttermost parts of the earth with signs and wonders following. This should be the aim of every believer.

The Great Commission is the primary mission of the local church. The key to world evangelism is to have a clear vision of our missions, goals and strategies.

Miracle evangelism must come from a fire within rather than being a program.

GREAT COMMISSION

Both Matthew and Mark recorded the final words of Jesus, The Great Commission.

Matthew 28:19,20 "Go therefore and make disciples of all the nations, baptizing them in the name of the Father and of the Son and of the Holy Spirit, teaching them to observe all things that I have commanded you; and lo, I am with you always, even to the end of the age." Amen.

Mark 16:15-18 And He said to them, "Go into all the world and preach the gospel to every creature. He who believes and is baptized will be saved; but he who does not believe will be condemned. And these signs will follow those who believe: in My name they will cast out demons; they will speak with new tongues; they will take up serpents; and if they drink anything deadly, it will by no means hurt them; they will lay hands on the sick, and they will recover."

"Go"

The love and compassion of Jesus for a lost world was revealed when Jesus commanded, "Go into all the world!"

Many have felt since they have not been sent by their local church as a missionary to a foreign land, the word "go" did not apply to them. They have reasoned, "I'm not called by God. I need to work to provide for my family's needs." They may even have reasoned, "God wants me to stay home and work and give so that others can go."

The words translated "go" in the Great Commission mean as you are going. Every believer is going about their daily life. Jesus' command to go wasn't limited to a select few who had a missionary calling. Instead, this command was and still is to all believers. It's to everyone who is going anywhere: to work; to school; to do the shopping; to visit friends, family or neighbors; wherever they are going to carry out the normal functions of everyday life.

Jesus said, "As you are going about the normal functions of life, you are to preach My gospel to every creature!" The Great Commission was given to every believer in Jesus Christ.

Evangelism is not something that is to be done by a select few. It's not something to be done just by those God has called to function as evangelists in the church.

Evangelism is not something we do once a week when it's time in our church program to go out witnessing. Evangelism is to become a life style. It's something we are to do all the time.

Into All the World

Jesus made it clear that the responsibility of the church for evangelism wasn't limited to their own city. They were to take the gospel to all the world. Not every believer will be led to some foreign land, but every believer is to be actively involved in world evangelism. Some are to send by giving, some are to go, but all are to witness everywhere they go.

The apostle Paul wrote,

2 Corinthians 10:16a ... to preach the gospel in the regions beyond you ...

The church must press into the regions beyond to reach the unreached souls. It must receive a renewed call for world evangelism. The supreme task of the church is the evangelism of the world.

The only way for the church to survive is soul winning. The church was born in the fires of miracle evangelism and is doomed when believers cease to reach the lost.

To Every Creature

God's plan for global harvest, for world evangelism, has never changed. We are still to go into all the world and preach the gospel to every creature allowing God to confirm His word with signs and wonders following, just as He promised.

Jesus made it clear that every believer was to begin right where they live. They were to reach their own cities with the gospel. However, they were not to stop there. They were to continue to take the gospel to others until everyone has heard of Jesus – to the ends of the earth.

The Great Commission

Acts 1:8 "But you shall receive power when the Holy Spirit has come upon you; and you shall be witnesses to Me in Jerusalem, and in all Judea and Samaria, and to the end of the earth."

Every Nation, Kindred, Tribe, People, Tongues

We are not to be restricted to our own areas, but we are to go beyond our regions to reach every nation, every kindred, tribe, people, tongue, creature and place.

The real success of the church is in the fulfillment of its mission. The awareness and consciousness of the mission is critical.

Preach Good News

When we preach the gospel, it must be done in the anointing of the Holy Spirit and accompanied with signs and wonders. It's not enough to just proclaim the word. God planned for there to be both a proclamation and a demonstration!

Luke 4:18 "The Spirit of the Lord is upon Me, because He has anointed Me to preach the gospel to the poor. He has sent Me to heal the brokenhearted, to preach deliverance to the captives and recovery of sight to the blind, to set at liberty those who are oppressed."

Matthew 24:14 "And this gospel of the kingdom will be preached in all the world as a witness to all the nations, and then the end will come."

Make Disciples

Not only are we to go and teach, we are to make disciples so that the Great Commission can be fulfilled. In God's plan, believers would multiply – not just add to their numbers.

When Jesus said in Matthew 28:19 that we are to make disciples of all nations, He revealed His plans for every believer to be trained and equipped to do His work through miracle evangelism.

2 Timothy 2:2 And the things that you have heard from me among many witnesses, commit these to faithful men who will be able to teach others also.

IMPORTANCE OF EVANGELISM

Evangelism is the only hope for this generation. There are no other answers for the problems of the world or for our personal problems other than the good news of Jesus Christ.

Each of us is saved because someone obeyed God and shared the gospel of Jesus Christ with us.

Our Responsibility

King Solomon gave us insight into our responsibilities to warn those facing death.

Proverbs 24:11,12 Deliver those who are drawn toward death, and hold back those stumbling to the slaughter.

If you say, "Surely we did not know this," does not He who weighs the hearts consider it? he who keeps your soul, does He not know it? and will He not render to each man according to his deeds?

If we don't warn those around us who are headed for hell, God will hold us accountable.

Our Guilt

The prophet Ezekiel warned us of our guilt if we knew to speak and said nothing.

Ezekiel 3:17-19 "Son of man, I have made you a watchman for the house of Israel; therefore hear a word from My mouth, and give them warning from Me: when I say to the wicked, 'You shall surely die,' and you give him no warning, nor speak to warn the wicked from his wicked way, to save his life, that same wicked man shall die in his iniquity; but his blood I will require at your hand. Yet, if you warn the wicked, and he does not turn from his wickedness, nor from his wicked way, he shall die in his iniquity; but you have delivered your soul."

Our Benefits

Isaiah told us of the benefits.

Isaiah 58:10 If you extend your soul to the hungry and satisfy the afflicted soul, then your light shall dawn in the darkness, and your darkness shall be as the noonday.

Our Priorities

On this earth, there are thousands of neglected villages and cities where millions of souls live seemingly untouched by the gospel. We, the body of Christ, must set our priorities right.

If the church is going to reach the lost with the gospel, all-out miracle evangelism must be given the top priority. Our soul-winning efforts must be expanded on every front.

The blood of martyrs has always been the seed sown for the harvest of souls into the kingdom of God. A great price has been paid by the sufferings and deaths of many believers in the past for us to be able to share the gospel to a lost and dying world.

The question today is:

What are we willing to do, to give, to take the gospel to our generation?

HEARTBEAT OF THE FATHER

When Jesus spoke the Great Commission, He was echoing the heartbeat of the Father. When we think of the sacrifice the Father made when He gave His Son, we know God's desire is for men to be made right with Himself.

Our Father-God has an aggressive compassion which reaches out to the whole world. His church must have the same heartbeat. And today, God is raising up an army which will move into the flow of His Spirit.

The Twelve Commissioned

Jesus sent out the twelve disciples with these instructions:

Matthew 10:7,8 "And as you go, preach, saying, 'The kingdom of heaven is at hand.' Heal the sick, cleanse the lepers, raise the dead, cast out demons. Freely you have received, freely give."

Parable of Lost Sheep

In the parable of the lost sheep, Jesus revealed the worth of one lost person.

Luke 15:3-7 So He spoke this parable to them, saying: "What man of you, having a hundred sheep, if he loses one of them, does not leave the ninety-nine in the wilderness, and go after the one which is lost until he finds it? And when he has found it, he lays it on his shoulders, rejoicing. And when he comes home, he calls together his friends and neighbors, saying to them, 'Rejoice with me, for I have found my sheep which was lost!'

"I say to you that likewise there will be more joy in heaven over one sinner who repents than over ninety-nine just persons who need no repentance."

Rejoicing in Heaven

The Holy Spirit through the apostle John, gave us a glimpse of a coming time of rejoicing in heaven. Notice, He wrote that the saved would come from every tribe, tongue, people, and nation.

Revelation 5:9 And they sang a new song, saying: "You are worthy to take the scroll, and to open its seals; for You were slain, and have redeemed us to God by Your blood out of every tribe and tongue and people and nation."

Miracle Evangelism

> Revelation 7:9,10 After these things I looked, and behold, a great multitude which no one could number, of all nations, tribes, peoples, and tongues, standing before the throne and before the Lamb, clothed with white robes, with palm branches in their hands, and crying out with a loud voice, saying, "Salvation belongs to our God who sits on the throne, and to the Lamb!"

NEW TESTAMENT STRATEGY

The New Testament strategy is a plan of total miracle evangelism. Total evangelism means the penetration of the entire world with the gospel.

It involves the believers of this generation confronting everyone in the world with the claims of Christ on his life.

Total Penetration

Early disciples began where they were in Jerusalem sharing Christ with everyone. They continued to spread the gospel into all Judea, then Samaria, and on to the uttermost parts of the earth.

Jesus' strategy is still total penetration of this world with His gospel.

Total Participation

Each church must accept responsibility and confront every person in their area personally with the gospel of the Lord Jesus Christ. Jesus said that every believer was to be a witness of Him.

> Acts 1:8 "But you shall receive power when the Holy Spirit has come upon you; and you shall be witnesses to Me in Jerusalem, and in all Judea and Samaria, and to the end of the earth."

Total penetration of our world with the gospel demands total participation of the membership of the local church in witnessing. They should enlist every believer in the work of reaching their vicinity for the Lord Jesus Christ.

Many Christians don't witness because they don't realize they need to witness. The believer must realize that witnessing for Jesus is not just an option for a Christian. It's a command. There are three things every minister must do to prepare believers for miracle evangelism. They must be:

➢ Enlightened
➢ Enlisted
➢ Equipped

The church today is to do exactly the same as the church Jesus left when He ascended into heaven.

The Great Commission

Mark 16:20 And they went out and preached everywhere, the Lord working with them and confirming the word through the accompanying signs. Amen.

Total Power

Paul's method of evangelism was the preaching of the gospel with a demonstration of the power of God.

1 Corinthians 2:1-5 And I, brethren, when I came to you, did not come with excellence of speech or of wisdom declaring to you the testimony of God. For I determined not to know anything among you except Jesus Christ and Him crucified. I was with you in weakness, in fear, and in much trembling. And my speech and my preaching were not with persuasive words of human wisdom, but in demonstration of the Spirit and of power, that your faith should not be in the wisdom of men but in the power of God.

Our efforts in evangelism must, like the apostle Paul's include a demonstration of the Spirit and of power through miracle evangelism!

QUESTIONS FOR REVIEW

1. What should be the primary mission of every local church?

2. Explain the meaning of the word "go" in the Great Commission as it's found in the original Greek New Testament. What does this mean in your life?

3. What is the New Testament strategy for winning the lost?

Lesson Two

Revival for Our Time!

God is moving one last time on the face of the earth. In this wave, the Father-God will reveal His manifested and tangible glory as never before. This end-time wave of God carries with it the faith for the miraculous which will produce the end-time harvest of souls.

The prophet Joel spoke of the pouring from the Holy Spirit for this time.

Joel 2:28 And it shall come to pass afterward that I will pour out My Spirit on all flesh; your sons and your daughters shall prophesy, your old men shall dream dreams, your young men shall see visions.

As the Father-God draws us into His presence, He will reveal His master plans for world evangelism.

As we behold the Father's glory, He will always lift our eyes to see the unreached nations.

Isaiah 33:17 Your eyes will see the King in His beauty; they will see the land that is very far off.

Every revival comes with a restored burden for the lost.

WAVE OF MIRACLE EVANGELISM

The greatest wave of miracle evangelism recorded in the New Testament began in Ephesus and swept across the province of Asia.

Acts 19:10 And this continued for two years, so that all who dwelt in Asia heard the word of the Lord Jesus, both Jews and Greeks.

This was total, "every creature," evangelism in action. It began as Paul arrived in Ephesus and ministered the baptism in the Holy Spirit to a group of believers to prepare them to be powerful, miracle-working witnesses for Jesus Christ.

Power to be Witnesses

Acts 19:1-7 And it happened, while Apollos was at Corinth, that Paul, having passed through the upper regions, came to Ephesus. And finding some disciples he said to them, "Did you receive the Holy Spirit when you believed?"

And they said to him, "We have not so much as heard whether there is a Holy Spirit."

And he said to them, "Into what then were you baptized?"

So they said, "Into John's baptism."

Miracle Evangelism

Then Paul said, "John indeed baptized with a baptism of repentance, saying to the people that they should believe on Him who would come after him, that is, on Christ Jesus."

When they heard this, they were baptized in the name of the Lord Jesus. And when Paul had laid hands on them, the Holy Spirit came upon them, and they spoke with tongues and prophesied. Now the men were about twelve in all.

Paul knew that if the province of Asia was to be reached with the gospel, every believer needed the power of the Holy Spirit.

Acts 1:8 But you shall receive power when the Holy Spirit has come upon you; and you shall be witnesses to Me in Jerusalem, and in all Judea and Samaria, and to the end of the earth.

Trained for Miracle Evangelism

Every believer needed the Holy Spirit to be His witnesses. They needed to be taught the word of God in such a powerful, practical way that they would be trained to do the works of Jesus. They needed to be trained for miracle evangelism.

Paul failed in his efforts to reach the Ephesians by himself. He then began to teach believers in the school of Tyrannus.

Acts 19:8-9 And he went into the synagogue and spoke boldly for three months, reasoning and persuading concerning the things of the kingdom of God. But when some were hardened and did not believe, but spoke evil of the Way before the multitude, he departed from them and withdrew the disciples, reasoning daily in the school of Tyrannus.

Paul's teaching in the school of Tyrannus over a two year period was so powerful, practical and effective that "all who dwelt in the province of Asia heard the word of the Lord Jesus, both Jews and Greeks."

Each one of the believers Paul had trained, apparently went out and trained others. They trained other believers all across the province of Asia. A mighty army was trained for miracle evangelism. As a result, there was a total saturation of the gospel to every person in that part of the world.

Miracles, Miracles, Miracles

Effective evangelism, according to God's pattern was always to be miracle evangelism. Miracles were in the center of this mighty wave of evangelism that swept across Asia.

Acts 19:11-17 Now God worked unusual miracles by the hands of Paul, so that even handkerchiefs or aprons were brought from his

Revival for Our Time!

body to the sick, and the diseases left them and the evil spirits went out of them.

Then some of the itinerant Jewish exorcists took it upon themselves to call the name of the Lord Jesus over those who had evil spirits, saying, "We adjure you by the Jesus whom Paul preaches."

Also there were seven sons of Sceva, a Jewish chief priest, who did so.

And the evil spirit answered and said, "Jesus I know, and Paul I know; but who are you?"

Then the man in whom the evil spirit was leaped on them, overpowered them, and prevailed against them, so that they fled out of that house naked and wounded.

This became known both to all Jews and Greeks dwelling in Ephesus; and fear fell on them all, and the name of the Lord Jesus was magnified.

Miracle evangelism always magnifies the Lord Jesus, and brings repentance and deliverance to the people.

Acts 19:18-20 And many who had believed came confessing and telling their deeds. Also, many of those who had practiced magic brought their books together and burned them in the sight of all. And they counted up the value of them, and it totaled fifty thousand pieces of silver. So the word of the Lord grew mightily and prevailed.

Through miracle evangelism, the word of the Lord grew to become the most important truth in the lives of believers. As they heard the word taught:

- Their faith exploded
- They believed the word
- They spoke the word
- They acted in obedience to the word
- They became mighty people of the word

As this happened, the word of God prevailed over the forces of spiritual darkness that had blinded the minds of the people.

A mighty wave of miracle evangelism swept across that whole part of the world and became a pattern of evangelism for us. Today, God is moving in mighty power on His church. He is preparing us for the same powerful, effective wave of miracle evangelism that began in Ephesus and swept in a mighty wave all across the province of Asia. God is moving on His church to prepare us for the great end-time harvest.

THE WAVES OF GOD

All through church history, God has moved in definite waves. A mighty wave began at Azuza Street in Los Angeles.

First Wave

In the first wave of this century, there was a revelation of Jesus.

> *Gifts*

There was an emphasis on the gifts of:

- Tongues
- Interpretation of tongues
- Prophecy

These gifts marked the Pentecostal and healing movements.

> *Ministries*

The prominent ministries were the evangelistic and healing ministries.

> *The Gates*

This move of God was typified when the children of Israel came through the gates of the Tabernacle.

Second Wave

In the second wave of God, during the charismatic renewal, there was a revelation of the Holy Spirit.

> *Gifts*

During this period there was an emphasis on:

- The word of wisdom
- The word of knowledge
- Discerning of spirits

> *Ministries*

The prominent ministries were those of the pastor and teacher.

> *The Courtyard*

This move of God was typified when the children of Israel ministered unto the Lord in the courts of the Tabernacle.

Third Wave

In the third wave of God, the one the church has entered now, there is a revelation of the Father-God.

➢ *Gifts*

The gifts of the Holy Spirit which are prominent during this move are:

➢ Working of miracles
➢ Gift of faith
➢ Gifts of healings

➢ *Ministries*

The outstanding ministries are those of the apostle and prophet. God is restoring the apostolic and prophetic ministries so that there will be a strong foundation for the church to do the works of Jesus.

➢ *Holy of Holies*

This move of God was typified when the High Priest of Israel entered into the Holy of Holies.

When believers enter into the presence of God in the Holy of Holies, they are developing a close, personal relationship with their heavenly Father.

There has never been a time when it was more important to hear what the Father speaks and to see what the Father is doing. Jesus said He only did what He saw the Father do. To follow Jesus in this, we must enter into the presence of God.

John 5:19 Then Jesus answered and said to them, "Most assuredly, I say to you, the Son can do nothing of Himself, but what He sees the Father do; for whatever He does, the Son also does in like manner."

Then Jesus instructed His disciples to do the same things He did.

John 14:12 "Most assuredly, I say to you, he who believes in Me, the works that I do he will do also; and greater works than these he will do, because I go to My Father."

END-TIME MOVE OF GOD

In the last days before Jesus' return, the glory of God will be manifested. There will be an intense presence of the Father in His glory and a mighty wave of His power demonstrated through signs and wonders.

Faith for Miracles

During this apostolic and prophetic age there will be:

➢ Strong moves of divine revelation
➢ Surges of His power with miracles, signs and wonders
➢ Daring faith for the impossible
➢ Supernatural confrontations with the power of Satan

➤ Heavy anointing and manifestations of God's glory

Isaiah 59:19 So shall they fear the name of the Lord from the west, and His glory from the rising of the sun; when the enemy comes in like a flood, the Spirit of the Lord will lift up a standard against him.

Harvest of Souls

All around the world, Christians are sensing that this is God's hour for global harvest. Major streams of Christianity are pointing toward the year 2000 as a target for fulfilling the Great Commission.

There is a fresh outbreak of dynamism in New Testament gifts with a renewed call for evangelism in this generation and decade.

There is a new surge of God's power and the phenomenon is no longer limited to Bible Schools or store-front missions. Christians are sensing an urgency in their heart for a Holy Ghost revival and a renewed zeal and challenge for miracle evangelism.

The missions battle cry has become more distinct. Total world evangelism will become a reality in this decade.

Jesus told His disciples that the fields were white unto harvest.

John 4:35 "Do you not say, 'There are still four months and then comes the harvest'? Behold, I say to you, lift up your eyes and look at the fields, for they are already white for harvest!"

This is harvest time in world evangelism!

Satan Hinders

Satan will do everything possible to hinder evangelism. Satan hates every form of evangelism. He hates:

➤ Personal evangelism
➤ Evangelists
➤ Evangelistic crusades
➤ Combined evangelistic efforts
➤ Miracle evangelism

Satan hates every move of God.

In Acts we have Paul's statement to King Agrippa concerning the commitment it takes to present the gospel in the face of Satan's opposition.

Acts 26:19-23 "Therefore, King Agrippa, I was not disobedient to the heavenly vision, but declared first to those in Damascus and in Jerusalem, and throughout all the region of Judea, and then to the Gentiles, that they should repent, turn to God, and do works befitting repentance. For these reasons the Jews seized me in the temple and tried to kill me.

"Therefore, having obtained help from God, to this day I stand, witnessing both to small and great, saying no other things than those which the prophets and Moses said would come—that the Christ would suffer, that He would be the first to rise from the dead, and would proclaim light to the Jewish people and to the Gentiles."

MIGHTY WARRIORS

God is raising up mighty warriors with a burden and vision for reaching the unreached. God wants us to be partners in the work which is nearest to the heart of the Father, the work of reaching the lost!

We can join with the mighty men of Israel of whom it was said, "The least were over a hundred, the greatest over a thousand."

1 Chronicles 12:14,15 These were from the sons of Gad, captains of the army; the least was over a hundred, and the greatest was over a thousand. These are the ones who crossed the Jordan in the first month, when it had overflowed all its banks; and they put to flight all those in the valleys, to the east and to the west.

Jesus spoke of the necessity for violent ones.

Matthew 11:12 "And from the days of John the Baptist until now the kingdom of heaven suffers violence, and the violent take it by force."

The writer of the book of Hebrews gave us a list of the violent acts of the mighty warriors of God.

Hebrews 11:33 ...who through faith subdued kingdoms, worked righteousness, obtained promises, stopped the mouths of lions ...

PREPARATION FOR WARFARE

Satan and his demons will not give up the souls of men without a battle.

We must train ourselves for war – for action. It's to be a spiritual battle.

God has revealed effective warfare tactics.

Wisdom from Above

We need more knowledge about this battle. In this combat, we need to know who our enemy is – their names, their methods, and where the battle is taking place.

Power of Holy Spirit

We need the power of the Holy Spirit in a way we have never possessed before. We need an understanding of God's will and God's strategy for victorious warfare.

Open Spiritual Eyes

God is revealing things to come and giving strict instructions on what we are to do. We must open our spiritual eyes and our hearts to be ready for battle.

Jesus said the gates of hell shall not prevail against His church.

Matthew 16:18 "And I also say to you that you are Peter, and on this rock I that you are Peter, and on this rock I will build My church, and the gates of Hades shall not prevail against it."

That means the gates of hell are not strong enough to stand against a direct onslaught or attack of the church.

The church is to be on the offensive. Instead of cowering behind its gates, the church is to be actively storming the strongholds of Satan.

Summary

The Spirit of God is calling the church to arms. God is sounding the trumpet in Zion. There is a great stirring in the house of God.

The devil and false prophets have declared war on the saints of God. But God has started preparation. He is raising up a mighty army which will go forth in the overcoming blood-bought victories. This army shall take the kingdom by force and bring a revival of miracle evangelism!

QUESTIONS FOR REVIEW

1. What are the three waves of God described in this lesson? Which of these waves of God are we now entering?

2. What spiritual gifts will be prominent in the third wave of God?

3. How are we to prepare ourselves for effective spiritual warfare in this end-time wave?

Lesson Three

The Church Triumphant

The church is the most powerful force on the face of the earth. The church Jesus said He would build was to be overcoming and triumphant.

Jesus said:
Matthew 16:18b "I will build My church, and the gates of Hades shall not prevail against it."

Many are trying to build churches using traditional patterns and methods. But we must lay aside our own traditions, and our own ideas, and and let Jesus reveal His plan for the body of Christ.

THE CHURCH RESTORED

God is moving one more time! The last wave of God is different from the past waves. This move is going to be highly visible for all to see and will turn the world up-side down! God is preparing an army of mighty warriors which cannot be stopped.

This is God's hour for global harvest. God is restoring the church to go and take the gospel to the ends of the earth.

We will be saying what the prophet Joel said when he wrote:

Joel 1:2 Hear this, you elders, and give ear, all you inhabitants of the land! Has anything like this happened in your days, or even in the days of your fathers?

When God restores His glory and tangible presence to the local church, people will no longer run to super-star ministries.

The masses will see and experience signs and wonders in the streets of our cities when God confirms His word through the hands of Spirit-filled believers. They will be drawn in great numbers to churches where the glory of God is manifested.

The glory of the Father will be present and powerful manifestations of His Spirit will result in great waves of miracle evangelism.

Old methods of evangelism have failed. But when believers flow in a demonstration of God's power and operate in miracle evangelism, the church will be the strong living organism it was meant to be.

In miracle evangelism, there will be ministry teams bringing healing to the sick and wounded. There will be a strong involvement of our youth when they join in reaping the harvest.

RESTORED FIVEFOLD MINISTRIES

For the church to be victorious, it must recognize the fivefold ministries ordained by Jesus and put them back in their proper position.

The apostle Paul said that Jesus gave gifts to the body of Christ. He gave leaders to the church.

Ephesians 4:8,10-13 Therefore He says: "When He ascended on high, He led captivity captive, and gave gifts to men."

And He Himself gave some to be apostles, some prophets, some evangelists, and some pastors and teachers, for the equipping of the saints for the work of ministry, for the edifying of the body of Christ, till we all come to the unity of the faith and the knowledge of the Son of God, to a perfect man, to the measure of the stature of the fullness of Christ.

Functions

Apostle, prophet, evangelist, pastor and teacher are not titles. They are functions. Each ministry function has an important part in edifying the body of Christ.

In their burden, they are evangelistic so the gospel will always be proclaimed

In their knowledge, they are teachers so they can instruct others in the word of God.

In their hearts, they are pastoral so they will care for the people.

In their vision, they are prophetic so they can lead God's people by His directions.

In their ministry, they are apostolic so they lay solid foundations based on the word of God. They will lead people in the ways of God.

Appointment

All of the five ministry gifts must be active and functioning in each local church if the believers are to be prepared for the work of service and built up to the maturity in the full measure of Christ. They are not appointed by man: they are appointed by God. This is His plan.

1 Corinthians 12:27,28 Now you are the body of Christ, and members individually. And God has appointed these in the church: First apostles, second prophets, third teachers, after that miracles, then gifts of healings, helps, administrations, varieties of tongues.

Servants

Just as Jesus ministered as a Servant, each of the fivefold ministries are to function as servants. They are called to be servants to the body of Christ.

John 13:3-5 Jesus, knowing that the Father had given all things into His hands, and that He had come from God and was going to God, rose from supper and laid aside His garments, took a towel and girded Himself. After that, He poured water into a basin and began to wash the disciples' feet, and to wipe them with the towel with which He was girded.

John 13:12-17 So when He had washed their feet, taken His garments, and sat down again, He said to them, "Do you know what I have done to you? You call me Teacher and Lord, and you say well, for so I am. If I then, your Lord and Teacher, have washed your feet, you also ought to wash one another's feet. For I have given you an example, that you should do as I have done to you. Most assuredly, I say to you, a servant is not greater than his master; nor is he who is sent greater than he who sent him. If you know these things, happy are you if you do them."

Equipping Every Believer

The fivefold ministry function is to equip the saints for the work of the ministry – to teach them to do works of Jesus. Their primary work is to:

➢ Perfect and complete the saints
➢ Prepare believers to do the works of ministry
➢ Preach the gospel of the kingdom

There are four stages of growth.

➢ Manhood – coming into the knowledge and wisdom of Jesus
➢ Priesthood – developing the character and attributes of Jesus
➢ Servanthood – acting in the authority and power of Jesus
➢ Fatherhood – doing the works and deeds of Jesus

APOSTLES

Definition

The Greek word for apostle is "apostolos." It means one sent out with authority to establish churches and one sent out to strengthen existing churches in the foundational doctrines and practical teachings of the word of God.

Functions

Apostles function in all the ministry gifts and operate in all the gifts of the Spirit.

Miracle Evangelism

Their ministry gifts will be recognized and received as a relationship in the Spirit to certain churches and other ministries. Signs, wonders and healing miracles will continually be manifested.

Apostles work closely with prophets in the ordaining of elders and in confirming the calling on certain believer's lives and establishing them into their ministry gifts. They will impart and release the gifts of the Holy Spirit through the laying on of hands.

Example

Paul and Barnabas are very good examples.

Acts 14:23 So when they had appointed elders in every church, and prayed with fasting, they commended them to the Lord in whom they had believed.

PROPHETS

Definition

The Greek word for prophet is "propheteuo." It means to foretell events and to speak under inspiration. A prophet is one who speaks for God.

Functions

The prophet ministers in a greater level of anointing than another believer who is operating in the gift of prophecy. A prophet will often minister together with an apostle in laying spiritual foundations and establishing and strengthening the churches.

Ephesians 2:20 ... having been built on the foundation of the apostles and prophets, Jesus Christ Himself being the chief cornerstone ...

Example

Agabus is a good example of a prophet.

Acts 21:10,11 And as we stayed many days, a certain prophet named Agabus came down from Judea. When he had come to us, he took Paul's belt, bound his own hands and feet, and said, "Thus says the Holy Spirit, 'So shall the Jews at Jerusalem bind the man who owns this belt, and deliver him into the hands of the Gentiles.'"

EVANGELISTS

Definition

The Greek word for evangelist is "evangelistes." The evangelist is in the front line of God's army. He or she has a burning desire to reach the unreached of this world.

Functions

Everywhere they go, they are witnessing and preaching the gospel as signs and wonders follow. They are actively involved in training other believers for miracle evangelism and mobilizing them into evangelistic outreach ministries.

Example

The best example of an evangelist is Philip.

Acts 8:5-8 Then Philip went down to the city of Samaria and preached Christ to them. And the multitudes with one accord heeded the things spoken by Philip, hearing and seeing the miracles which he did. For unclean spirits, crying with a loud voice, came out of many who were possessed; and many who were paralyzed and lame were healed. And there was great joy in that city.

The primary work of the evangelist, like those who function in the other ministry giftings, is to equip the saints for the work of the ministry. The primary work of the evangelist is not to do all the work of evangelism, but to train believers to do the work of evangelism.

PASTORS

Definition

The Greek word for pastor is "poimen," and is translated as shepherd. A shepherd is one who tends herds or flocks. He guides as well as feeds the flocks. He is an overseer.

Functions

The function of the pastor is to take care of, oversee, lead, and train the people. He will have a personal relationship with them, and will love them even to the point of giving his life for them.

Example

Jesus is an example of all of the ministry giftings. We often picture Him as the Good Shepherd, and He is the best example of the pastor.

John 10:4 And when he brings out his own sheep, he goes before them; and the sheep follow him, for they know his voice.

John 10:11 "I am the good shepherd. The good shepherd gives His life for the sheep."

TEACHERS

Definition

"Didaskalo" is the Greek word which is translated, teacher. A teacher is one who instructs and by his teaching causes others to learn.

Matthew 28:19,20 "Go therefore and make disciples of all the nations, baptizing them in the name of the Father and of the Son and of the Holy Spirit, teaching them to observe all things that I have

Miracle Evangelism

commanded you; and lo, I am with you always, even to the end of the age." Amen.

Functions

A teacher is one who points the way, directs, informs, and shows the ways of the Lord. His primary goal is to instruct the body of Christ. It's his or her responsibility to teach under the anointing of the Holy Spirit.

1 Corinthians 2:13 These things we also speak, not in words which man's wisdom teaches but which the Holy Spirit teaches, comparing spiritual things with spiritual.

Example

Timothy is a good example of the teacher.

1 Timothy 2:7 ... for which I was appointed a preacher and an apostle–I am speaking the truth in Christ and not lying–a teacher of the Gentiles in faith and truth.

The apostle John wrote these words to a teacher.

1 John 2:27 But the anointing which you have received from Him abides in you, and you do not need that anyone teach you; but as the same anointing teaches you concerning all things, and is true, and is not a lie, and just as it has taught you, you will abide in Him.

RESTORED GOSPEL

The gospel of Jesus Christ is to be presented with signs and wonders.

T. L. Osborn wrote,

It is this gospel of the kingdom preached in the power of God, confirmed by signs and wonders and divers miracles which produces the greatest evangelistic triumph in any generation. Whether it was Peter in traditional Jerusalem, Philip in immoral Samaria, Paul in pagan Melita, the same results are seen: the gospel preached in signs and wonders and multitudes added to the church.

The apostle Paul wrote:
1 Corinthians 2:1-5 I was with you in weakness, in fear, and in much trembling. And my speech and my preaching were not with persuasive words of human wisdom, but in demonstration of the Spirit and of power, that your faith should not be in the wisdom of men but in the power of God.

1 Corinthians 4:20 For the kingdom of God is not in word but in power.

THE LOCAL CHURCH

The local church is to be a center for the manifestation of His glory, a place for the gifts to flow so the world can be reached. This is where disciples are to be discipled, trained and sent to do the works of Jesus.

In God's plan, it was to be in the local church where the apostles, prophets, and the other ministry gifts were to operate in training every believer for the work of the ministry.

God cannot use a church which is in rebellion by holding on to their traditions even when they are contrary to New Testament patterns.

God will use a church which understands the new move of God in team ministry – a church where fivefold ministry leaders work together to equip every believer for the work of the ministry.

In these forceful New Testament churches, the glory of God will be manifested and all believers will be trained and released into powerful, effective miracle evangelism.

*For more information on the subject of the church read **The Church Triumphant** by A.L. and Joyce Gill.*

QUESTIONS FOR REVIEW

1. Next to God, what is the most powerful force on the face of the earth?

2. In this end-time move of God, what will draw people to the churches?

3. In order for the church to be victorious, what needs to be restored to the church?

Lesson Four

Authority of the Believer

Satan has blinded the spiritual eyes of the lost of this world. Millions, held in spiritual darkness through spirits of deception and false religions, are heading for an eternity in hell.

If we are to be effective in reaching the lost, we must also be trained for powerful spiritual warfare so that we may set the captives free.

Many have tried to enter spiritual warfare without a revelation of the authority of the believer. They have been overwhelmed with thoughts of how powerful the devil and his demons are. They have been intimidated and have become preoccupied with what they believe is an intense life-and-death struggle. It's important that believers are taught about their overcoming spiritual authority before they are taught about spiritual warfare.

With a revelation of who they are in Jesus Christ, their authority in the name of Jesus, and of the overcoming power of His blood and the word of God, believers are venturing forth with a new boldness to enter into the strongholds of the devil and to set the captives free.

An understanding of the authority of the believer and of the powerful weapons of our warfare, will prepare us for effective miracle evangelism in these last days.

POWER AND AUTHORITY OF BELIEVERS

Authority Given to Mankind

God created man in His own image and gave him authority (dominion) to rule over everything in this earth.

Genesis 1:26 Then God said, "Let Us make man in Our image, according to Our likeness; let them have dominion over the fish of the sea, over the birds of the air, and over the cattle, over all the earth and over every creeping thing that creeps on the earth."

After the war in heaven, Satan was cast down to this earth. He watched when God created man and breathed into him the breath of life. He watched when God created woman from a part of Adam's side and gave to these new creatures dominion over every living thing over the face of the earth. Since Satan was living in the earth, this dominion includes authority over Satan and all of his demon followers.

Miracle Evangelism

Purpose of Creation

God created man and woman and gave them authority over the earth. God didn't give authority to man until He had created Eve. God said they were to have dominion. God planned that men and women should walk in dominion and authority together on the earth.

Adam Given Free Will

Genesis 2:16,17 And the Lord God commanded the man, saying, "Of every tree of the garden you may freely eat; but of the tree of the knowledge of good and evil you shall not eat, for in the day that you eat of it you shall surely die."

God gave Adam a free will. He had the power to choose between obeying or disobeying God. Man's volition was to be tested in the garden of Eden between obedience and disobedience.

Authority in Action

Genesis 2:19 Out of the ground the Lord God formed every beast of the field and every bird of the air, and brought them to Adam to see what he would call them. And whatever Adam called each living creature, that was its name.

As Adam named all of the animals, we see him operating in his God-given authority on this earth.

Satan Hated Mankind

Satan hated mankind because they were created in the image of God.

- They looked like God.
- They walked like God.
- They talked like God.

All the hatred which Satan in his rebellion had toward God was turned toward those God-like creatures called man and woman.

Satan's Fear

It is extremely important to Satan that we don't discover and walk in the authority that God has given us.

Genesis 1:28 Then God blessed them, and God said to them, "Be fruitful and multiply; fill the earth and subdue it; have dominion over the fish of the sea, over the birds of the air, and over every living thing that moves on the earth."

THE AUTHORITY LOST

The Fall of Man

When Adam and Eve disobeyed God and lost their God-given rights, they lost the authority they had been created to have.

➢ *Deception*

Satan was experienced in deception. He had deceived the angels in heaven. One-third of the angels followed him in rebellion.

Genesis 2:17 "but of the tree of the knowledge of good and evil you shall not eat, for in the day that you eat of it you shall surely die."

Genesis 3:1 Now the serpent was more cunning than any beast of the field which the Lord God had made. And he said to the woman, "Has God indeed said, 'You shall not eat of every tree of the garden'?"

Satan disguised himself and came into the garden unnoticed. He had no right in the garden and Adam could have cast him out if he had recognized him.

➢ *Satan's Lie*

Satan misquoted God's words to twist them into deception.

Genesis 3:2-6 And the woman said to the serpent, "We may eat the fruit of the trees of the garden; but of the fruit of the tree which is in the midst of the garden, God has said, 'You shall not eat it, nor shall you touch it, lest you die.'"

And the serpent said to the woman, "You will not surely die. For God knows that in the day you eat of it your eyes will be opened, and you will be like God, knowing good and evil."

So when the woman saw that the tree was good for food, that it was pleasant to the eyes, and a tree desirable to make one wise, she took of its fruit and ate. She also gave to her husband with her, and he ate.

In verse three, Eve added "touch" to what God had said.

Satan told Eve "You will not surely die." He told her their eyes would be opened and they would be like God.

➢ *Sin*

Adam and Eve stopped following what God had said and started to follow their natural senses and listened to Satan. Satan tricked and defeated them. When they sinned, they lost the nature of God and they stood naked without the glory of God.

Satan's Winnings

When Adam and Eve sinned, they surrendered their God-given authority to Satan. In this way, he again became the

Miracle Evangelism

god of this world, the ruler of this world, and the prince of the power of the air.

Over a period of time, people who were created to walk and talk like God were:

➢ blind, begging beside the roads
➢ bound with spirits of infirmity
➢ possessed with legions of demons
➢ had faces and bodies eaten away by leprosy
➢ leaders blinded by deception and religious traditions

FROM CROSS TO THRONE

Jesus paid the price for our sins by shedding His blood and dying on the cross. He delivered all our sin, sicknesses, diseases and infirmities into the place of torment.

Colossians 2:14 ...having wiped out the handwriting of requirements that was against us, which was contrary to us. And He has taken it out of the way, having nailed it to the cross.

In the Spirit World

Jesus carried our sins to the depths of this earth and suffered the torment of hades and hell on our behalf. As He helplessly descended into the depths of the pit, He delivered every sin which has ever been committed.

Psalms 88:3,7 For my soul is full of troubles, and my life draws near to the grave. Your wrath lies heavy upon me, and You have afflicted me with all Your waves. Selah

Devil and Demons Defeated

When Jesus delivered our sin into the deepest parts of the earth, the power of God came on Him.

Acts 2:27 ... because You will not leave my soul in Hades, nor will You allow Your Holy One to see corruption.

The gates of hell could not prevail against Him. He took the keys of death, hell and of the grave, away from Satan.

Colossians 2:15 Having disarmed principalities and powers, He made a public spectacle of them, triumphing over them in it.

Jesus disarmed and stripped Satan and his demons of all their authority.

The Resurrection

When Jesus rose from the dead, Satan and his demons were forever defeated.

Ephesians 1:19-21 ... and what is the exceeding greatness of His power toward us who believe, according to the working of His mighty power which He worked in Christ when He raised Him from the dead and seated Him at His right hand in the heavenly places, far above all principality and power and might and dominion, and every name that is named, not only in this age but also in that which is to come.

Entered Heaven

Jesus entered heaven and victoriously went into the Father's presence.

Psalms 24:7-10 Lift up your heads, O you gates! And be lifted up, you everlasting doors! And the King of glory shall come in.

Who is this King of glory? The Lord strong and mighty, the Lord mighty in battle.

Lift up your heads, O you gates! And lift them up, you everlasting doors! And the King of glory shall come in.

Who is this King of glory? The Lord of hosts, He is the King of glory. Selah

VICTORY

Jesus had the keys of authority which He had taken back from Satan.

Revelation 1:18 "I am He who lives, and was dead, and behold, I am alive forevermore. Amen. And I have the keys of Hades and of Death."

Keys Given to Man

Jesus gave these keys of authority to His church. As a new creation, man's authority has been restored on this earth.

Matthew 16:18,19 "And I also say to you that you are Peter, and on this rock I will build My church, and the gates of Hades shall not prevail against it. And I will give you the keys of the kingdom of heaven, and whatever you bind on earth will be bound in heaven, and whatever you loose on earth will be loosed in heaven."

Authority Restored

Once again, regenerated mankind has been restored to his original place of authority on this earth.

Luke 10:19 Behold, I give you the authority to trample on serpents and scorpions, and over all the power of the enemy, and nothing shall by any means hurt you.

Jesus' Work Complete

Jesus sat down at the Father's right hand, because His redemptive work for mankind was complete. His work on earth was completed.

Psalms 110:1 The Lord said to my Lord, "Sit at My right hand, till I make Your enemies Your footstool."

Man's Work Begins

Now it's the work of every believer as part of the body of Christ, to use the authority for God's original purpose. God's original purpose was for men and women to have dominion on the earth.

Ephesians 1:18-23 ... the eyes of your understanding being enlightened; that you may know what is the hope of His calling, what are the riches of the glory of His inheritance in the saints, and what is the exceeding greatness of His power toward us who believe, according to the working of His mighty power which He worked in Christ when He raised Him from the dead and seated Him at His right hand in the heavenly places, far above all principality and power and might and dominion, and every name that is named, not only in this age but also in that which is to come.

And He put all things under His feet, and gave Him to be head over all things to the church, which is His body, the fullness of Him who fills all in all.

Satan and his followers are defeated. They are under the feet of Jesus. We are the body of Christ. That means Satan and his demons are under our feet.

Ephesians 1:22 And He put all things under His feet, and gave Him to be head over all things to the church ...

Romans 16:20 And the God of peace will crush Satan under your feet shortly. The grace of our Lord Jesus Christ be with you. Amen.

To be under one's feet is a picture of being totally conquered, defeated and subdued. On the opposite side, it's a picture of absolute authority.

Jesus Is Waiting

Jesus is seated at the right hand of His Father, waiting for believers to discover their restored authority. Then they will arise and demonstrate that Satan and all his demons are defeated as they put them under their feet.

Jesus is waiting for us to complete our job of miracle evangelism on this earth through effective spiritual warfare.

Hebrews 10:12,13 But this Man, after He had offered one sacrifice for sins forever, sat down at the right hand of God, from that time waiting till His enemies are made His footstool.

Believers Should Rule

Jesus came to restore to mankind the rightful rulership lost to Satan.

We have been translated into the kingdom of the Son. We are to rule and reign in His kingdom here on this earth.

Authority of the Believer

Colossians 1:13-18 He has delivered us from the power of darkness and translated us into the kingdom of the Son of His love, in whom we have redemption through His blood, the forgiveness of sins.

He is the image of the invisible God, the firstborn over all creation. For by Him all things were created that are in heaven and that are on earth, visible and invisible, whether thrones or dominions or principalities or powers. All things were created through Him and for Him. And He is before all things, and in Him all things consist. And He is the head of the body, the church, who is the beginning, the firstborn from the dead, that in all things He may have the preeminence.

Jesus is the Head and we are His body. As His body, we are "His feet."

Walking in Authority

Isaiah 54:14-17 "In righteousness you shall be established; you shall be far from oppression, for you shall not fear; and from terror, for it shall not come near you. Indeed they shall surely assemble, but not because of Me. Whoever assembles against you shall fall for your sake.

"Behold, I have created the blacksmith who blows the coals in the fire, who brings forth an instrument for his work; and I have created the spoiler to destroy. No weapon formed against you shall prosper, and every tongue which rises against you in judgment you shall condemn. This is the heritage of the servants of the Lord, and their righteousness is from Me," says the Lord.

Forceful Evangelism

Today, as believers discover their restored authority, there is arising a mighty army of believers, who are committed to forcibly advancing the kingdom of God, and setting the captives free. They are committed to taking the gospel to every creature. They have discovered their weapons are mighty through God to the pulling down of strongholds. They are committed to aggressive, militant, miracle evangelism.

Together, with Jesus as the Commander-in-Chief of His army, we are boldly saying, "This gospel of the kingdom will be preached in all the world as a witness to all the nations, and then the end will come."

For in-depth study on the subject of the believer's authority, read **The Authority of the Believer** *and the book,* **Destined for Dominion** *by A.L. Gill.*

Miracle Evangelism

QUESTIONS FOR REVIEW

1. What knowledge should be imparted before a believer is taught about spiritual warfare?

2. Why does Satan hate mankind?

3. This lesson describes a major loss that Adam and Eve suffered when they disobeyed and sinned against God. Describe that loss.

4. What was God's plan for restoring this "loss" to mankind?

Lesson Five

Militant Evangelism

INTRODUCTION

Every believer who has a revelation of the authority he or she has in Jesus Christ will be on the cutting edge of miracle evangelism. He or she will boldly bombard the gates of hell, setting people free from the control of Satan.

This end-time army will victoriously overcome demon powers and gather the precious end-time harvest into the hands of God.

Floods of Demons

There will be floods of demons trying to block this harvest. Their purpose will be to overthrow God's plan to raise up a mature and glorious church destined to win the nations with the good news of Jesus Christ.

Raising a Standard

Satan has his plans, but God has a better plan. Isaiah wrote that when the enemy comes in like a flood, the Lord will raise up a standard against him.

We are that standard.

Isaiah 59:19 So shall they fear the name of the Lord from the west, and His glory from the rising of the sun; when the enemy comes in like a flood, the Spirit of the Lord will lift up a standard against him.

Regional Spirits

There are demon spirits over:

- nations
- regions
- districts
- families

The demon Prince of Persia is an example of this. We are told that the ruling principality of Persia withstood the angel of the Lord from bringing the answers to Daniel's prayer. Later Michael, one of the chief heavenly princes, was sent to assist him in the battle.

Daniel 10:13 "But the prince of the kingdom of Persia withstood me twenty-one days; and behold, Michael, one of the chief princes, came to help me, for I had been left alone there with the kings of Persia."

WARFARE IN EVANGELISM

When we begin to evangelize, we are coming against the strongholds of the devil. We must operate in our God-given rights of binding and loosing so that the captives can go free.

We should expect to come into direct confrontation with principal rulers.

Therefore, it's important that we:

➢ Know about the strong man
➢ Exercise our authority
➢ Possess the occupied lands
➢ Know how to enter into warfare!

Hindering Spirits

There are unseen spirit-forces in Satan's army whose primary job is to hinder the expansion of the gospel. Through lack of knowledge as intercessors, we often fail to directly attack the unseen forces of darkness.

1 Thessalonians 2:18 Therefore we wanted to come to you–even I, Paul, time and again–but Satan hindered us.

Spiritual Blindness

Satan has blinded the hearts of the unbelievers from receiving the gospel.

Believers must break this spiritual blindness by binding the demons which are ruling their lives. They must also loose the light of the gospel to shine on them.

2 Corinthians 4:4 ...whose minds the god of this age has blinded, who do not believe, lest the light of the gospel of the glory of Christ, who is the image of God, should shine on them.

Binding Strong Man

Jesus taught that we must first bind the strong men which are the principalities and powers which are ruling in territories, nations, regions, areas, families and individuals.

Matthew 12:29 "Or else how can one enter a strong man's house and plunder his goods, unless he first binds the strong man? And then he will plunder his house."

Matthew 18:18 "Assuredly, I say to you, whatever you bind on earth will be bound in heaven, and whatever you loose on earth will be loosed in heaven."

We are to operate in the gift of discerning of spirits to recognize the ruling spirits, and then to bind and cast them out.

1 Corinthians 12:7-11 But the manifestation of the Spirit is given to each one for the profit of all: for to one is given the word of wisdom through the Spirit, to another the word of knowledge through the same Spirit, to another faith by the same Spirit, to another gifts of healings by the same Spirit, to another the working of miracles, to another prophecy, to another discerning of spirits, to another different kinds of tongues, to another the interpretation of tongues. But one and the same Spirit works all these things, distributing to each one individually as He wills.

Spiritual Wrestling

Spiritual warfare often involves persistent wrestling in the spirit realm. The answers to our needs and prayers are not always easily attained. There are times when we must endure hardship as a good soldier of Jesus Christ.

The apostle Paul wrote of this.
Ephesians 6:12 For we do not wrestle against flesh and blood, but against principalities, against powers, against the rulers of the darkness of this age, against spiritual hosts of wickedness in the heavenly places.

David wrote words of encouragement for the times of wrestling.

Psalms 91:11,13 For He shall give His angels charge over you, to keep you in all your ways.

You shall tread upon the lion and the cobra, the young lion and the serpent you shall trample under foot.

Ministering Angels

A mighty army of angels is available to enter into the warfare with us. Jesus said He could pray to the Father and He would send the angels.

Matthew 26:53 "Or do you think that I cannot now pray to My Father, and He will provide Me with more than twelve legions of angels?"

The angels want to be sent into warfare as ministering spirits on our behalf.

Hebrews 1:14 Are they not all ministering spirits sent forth to minister for those who will inherit salvation?

As we speak the word of God, the angels respond and move into action on our behalf.

Psalms 103:20 Bless the Lord, you His angels, who excel in strength, who do His word, heeding the voice of His word.

EXAMPLES OF WARFARE

War in Heaven

There are examples of spiritual warfare in the Bible. One example is the warfare between the demon Prince of Persia and Michael and the angels. Another is the description of the battle in heaven between Michael and Satan.

Revelation 12:7-11 And war broke out in heaven: Michael and his angels fought against the dragon; and the dragon and his angels fought, but they did not prevail, nor was a place found for them in heaven any longer.

So the great dragon was cast out, that serpent of old, called the Devil and Satan, who deceives the whole world; he was cast to the earth, and his angels were cast out with him.

Then I heard a loud voice saying in heaven, "Now salvation, and strength, and the kingdom of our God, and the power of His Christ have come, for the accuser of our brethren, who accused them before our God day and night, has been cast down. And they overcame him by the blood of the Lamb and by the word of their testimony, and they did not love their lives to the death."

Prince of Persia

The weapons provided by the Lord are spiritual weapons for a war which is raging above us in the heavenlies. This war is between two armies of spiritual beings with great power, each demanding equal access to the sons of men.

Angelic beings warred against the demon Prince of Persia.

The delay wasn't from God's unwillingness to answer Daniel's prayer. A demon prince had intercepted the answer in the heavenlies.

Daniel 10:12,13 Then he said to me, "Do not fear, Daniel, for from the first day that you set your heart to understand, and to humble yourself before your God, your words were heard; and I have come because of your words. But the prince of the kingdom of Persia withstood me twenty-one days; and behold, Michael, one of the chief princes, came to help me, for I had been left alone there with the kings of Persia."

Amalek

Amalek is an example of what happens in the spirit realm when we pray. Amalek and his armies represent Satan and his angels. Joshua and his army represent Michael and the heavenly angels. Moses, standing on the hill with the rod extended, represents prayer warriors in intercessory prayer.

The war in the heavenlies is won by those below.

Revelation 12:11 And they overcame him by the blood of the Lamb and by the word of their testimony, and they did not love their lives to the death.

Exodus 17:8-12 Now Amalek came and fought with Israel in Rephidim.

And Moses said to Joshua, "Choose us some men and go out, fight with Amalek. Tomorrow I will stand on the top of the hill with the rod of God in my hand."

So Joshua did as Moses said to him, and fought with Amalek. And Moses, Aaron, and Hur went up to the top of the hill.

And so it was, when Moses held up his hand, that Israel prevailed; and when he let down his hand, Amalek prevailed. But Moses' hands became heavy; so they took a stone and put it under him, and he sat on it. And Aaron and Hur supported his hands, one on one side, and the other on the other side; and his hands were steady until the going down of the sun.

So Joshua defeated Amalek and his people with the edge of the sword.

Then the Lord said to Moses, "Write this for a memorial in the book and recount it in the hearing of Joshua, that I will utterly blot out the remembrance of Amalek from under heaven." And Moses built an altar and called its name, The-Lord-Is-My-Banner; for he said, "Because the Lord has sworn: the Lord will have war with Amalek from generation to generation."

Travailing in Prayer

Just as it's sometimes necessary to wrestle against the forces of darkness, it's sometimes necessary to travail in prayer to gain the victory.

The Holy Spirit helps us in intercessory prayer in groanings which cannot be uttered.

Romans 8:26,27 Likewise the Spirit also helps in our weaknesses. For we do not know what we should pray for as we ought, but the Spirit Himself makes intercession for us with groanings which cannot be uttered. Now He who searches the hearts knows what the mind of the Spirit is, because He makes intercession for the saints according to the will of God.

Effective warfare prayers are bold prayers of faith which are based on an absolute confidence that we will win.

GUERRILLA TRAINING

Theater of War

Paul encouraged the believers to put on the whole armor of God and go to battle with the enemy.

Ephesians 6:10-17 Finally, my brethren, be strong in the Lord and in the power of His might. Put on the whole armor of God, that you may be able to stand against the wiles of the devil. For we do not wrestle against flesh and blood, but against principalities, the darkness of this age, against spiritual hosts of wickedness in the heavenly places.

Miracle Evangelism

> Therefore take up the whole armor of God, that you may be able to withstand in the evil day, and having done all, to stand. Stand therefore, having girded your waist with truth, having put on the breastplate of righteousness,and having shod your feet with the preparation of the gospel of peace; above all, taking the shield of faith with which you will be able to quench all the fiery darts of the wicked one. And take the helmet of salvation, and the sword of the Spirit, which is the word of God;

He gave the battle cry in verse 18.

> Ephesians 6:18 praying always with all prayer and supplication in the Spirit, being watchful to this end with all perseverance and supplication for all the saints.

The warfare is in the spirit realm. God's angels and Satan with his demons are pitted in a death-struggle of global proportions. They are striving for the minds and souls of men and women.

The believer's weaponry to take these nations from the kingdom of darkness into the kingdom of light is intercessory prayer.

> 2 Corinthians 10:3-5 For though we walk in the flesh, we do not war according to the flesh. For the weapons of our warfare are not carnal but mighty in God for pulling down strongholds, casting down arguments and every high thing that exalts itself against the knowledge of God, bringing every thought into captivity to the obedience of Christ.

> Mark 3:27 No one can enter a strong man's house and plunder his goods, unless he first binds the strong man, and then he will plunder his house.

Jesus has given us the keys of the kingdom and He expects us to violently take our cities and the nations of the world away from the enemy by binding the strong man over the region. This is done only through intercessory prayer.

Prayer is the language of war!

Prayer and Evangelism

When we pray for the harvest, we are to pray for the nations of the world and their leaders. We are to pray for a peaceful environment conducive for miracle evangelism.

When Paul wrote to Timothy, he gave us an example of how we are to pray.

> 1 Timothy 2:1-4 Therefore I exhort first of all that supplications, prayers, intercessions, and giving of thanks be made for all men, for kings and all who are in authority, that we may lead a quiet and peaceable life in all godliness and reverence. For this is good and acceptable in the sight of God our Savior, who desires all men to be saved and to come to the knowledge of the truth.

Opening Blind Eyes

Intercessory prayer should be directed to the throne of God so that the blindness of the hearts of men may be removed. We are to come against the spiritual darkness which blinds the unbelievers.

2 Corinthians 4:3-6 But even if our gospel is veiled, it is veiled to those who are perishing, whose minds the god of this age has blinded, who do not believe, lest the light of the gospel of the glory of Christ, who is the image of God, should shine on them. For we do not preach ourselves, but Christ Jesus the Lord, and ourselves your servants for Jesus' sake. For it is the God who commanded light to shine out of darkness who has shone in our hearts to give the light of the knowledge of the glory of God in the face of Jesus Christ.

We have authority to strip away the veil and let the light of the gospel shine.

Tearing Down Strongholds

God desires to build a praying army which uses intercessory prayer to pull down the strongholds of the devil. He desires an army which will bind the demon spirits which hinder the harvest, and loose the Holy Spirit to draw the lost to Christ.

He desires an army which will beseech the Lord of the harvest to send out more laborers into the harvest field, and dispatch the body of angels to battle against the devil and his angels.

Isaiah 43:5-7 Fear not, for I am with you; I will bring your descendants from the east, and gather you from the west; I will say to the north, 'Give them up!' And to the south, 'Do not keep them back!' Bring My sons from afar, and My daughters from the ends of the earth – everyone who is called by My name, whom I have created for My glory; I formed him, yes, I have made him.

Reaping the Harvest

Having won the war in the spirit world, over each territory, we must then move in with the gospel and through miracle evangelism reap a harvest of souls.

QUESTIONS FOR REVIEW

1. Briefly list the steps of effective spiritual warfare in militant evangelism.

2. How are we to pray if we are to be effective in militant miracle evangelism?

3. How do we get angels to minister on our behalf?

Lesson Six

Releasing the Global Harvest

There are two important prerequisites to global harvest. They are prayer and praise.

PRAYER

With Commitment

We should have a set time for prayer and then continue in a spirit of worship and intercession throughout the day.

Peter and John had a set time for prayer, the ninth hour.

Acts 3:1 Now Peter and John went up together to the temple at the hour of prayer, the ninth hour.

Fervently

The apostle James taught that it's those who pray violently which press into kingdom possibilities.

James 5:16 Confess your trespasses to one another, and pray for one another, that you may be healed. The effective, fervent prayer of a righteous man avails much.

Specifically

Too often, we pray in generalities. This doesn't involve a lot of faith. When we ask specifically for this or that, we are having faith for certain things to happen.

Matthew 16:19 "And I will give you the keys of the kingdom of heaven, and whatever you bind on earth will be bound in heaven, and whatever you loose on earth will be loosed in heaven."

In Unity

One of the reasons for the effectiveness of the early church was that they prayed in one accord – in unity.

Acts 4:24a So when they heard that, they raised their voice to God with one accord ...

Persistently

Jesus taught that persistent prayer brings results.

Luke 11:9 "And I say to you, ask, and it will be given to you; seek, and you will find; knock, and it will be opened to you."

Boldly

When we know beyond any doubt that something is God's will, we can pray with great boldness.

For example, we know that it's always God's will for the lost to be saved. We can pray specifically for the salvation of a particular person.

2 Peter 3:9 The Lord is not slack concerning His promise, as some count slackness, but is longsuffering toward us, not willing that any should perish but that all should come to repentance.

Expectantly

Faith expects. When we pray with faith, we expect the answer to our prayers to come.

Mark 11:23,24 "For assuredly, I say to you, whoever says to this mountain, 'Be removed and be cast into the sea,' and does not doubt in his heart, but believes that those things he says will come to pass, he will have whatever he says. Therefore I say to you, whatever things you ask when you pray, believe that you receive them, and you will have them.

In Forgiveness

vs. 25,26 And whenever you stand praying, if you have anything against anyone, forgive him, that your Father in heaven may also forgive you your trespasses. But if you do not forgive, neither will your Father in heaven forgive your trespasses."

PRAISE AND WORSHIP

What Is Praise?

Praise is an expression of heartfelt gratitude and thanksgiving to God for all He has done for us. It's a physical and vocal expression of our sincere appreciation of God meaning:

- ➢ To speak well of
- ➢ To express admiration for
- ➢ To compliment
- ➢ To commend
- ➢ To congratulate
- ➢ To applaud
- ➢ To eulogize
- ➢ To extol

What Is Worship?

Worship is the highest form of praise. Worship is going beyond the thoughts of all His wonderful blessings to us. We are expressing and commending God for Himself, for His character, attributes and perfection.

- ➢ To express reverence
- ➢ To have a sense of awe
- ➢ To bow low before the object of worship

➤ To esteem the worth
➤ To give place to

Communion with God

All inferiority, depression and self-consciousness leaves when we begin to praise and worship the Lord. This gives the believer freedom to enter boldly into God's presence and communicate with Him.

When we enter into high praise, He will often draw us into His glory. The glory of God is the manifestation, expression, and the personification of the nature and the life of God. When the glory cloud comes, the gifts of the Holy Spirit will be manifested in a greater intensity causing instant healings and deliverance.

2 Chronicles 5:13,14 ... indeed it came to pass, when the trumpeters and singers were as one, to make one sound to be heard in praising and thanking the Lord, and when they lifted up their voice with the trumpets and cymbals and instruments of music, and praised the Lord, saying: "For He is good, for His mercy endures forever," that the house, the house of the Lord, was filled with a cloud, so that the priests could not continue ministering because of the cloud; for the glory of the Lord filled the house of God.

A Flowing River

When we praise and worship God, His presence flows in like a river and His throne is built in our midst. This is the river of God which Ezekiel wrote flows from the throne room of God.

Ezekiel 47:1,9,12 Then he brought me back to the door of the temple; and there was water, flowing from under the threshold of the temple toward the east, for the front of the temple faced east; the water was flowing from under the right side of the temple, south of the altar.

And it shall be that every living thing that moves, wherever the rivers go, will live. There will be a very great multitude of fish, because these waters go there; for they will be healed, and everything will live wherever the river goes.

Along the bank of the river, on this side and that, will grow all kinds of trees used for food; their leaves will not wither, and their fruit will not fail. They will bear fruit every month, because their water flows from the sanctuary. Their fruit will be for food, and their leaves for medicine.

When God's people come together in unrestrained praise and intimate worship, there will always be a flow of the gifts of His spirit, a flow of miracles, signs and wonders.

John 7:37,38 On the last day, that great day of the feast, Jesus stood and cried out, saying, "If anyone thirsts, let him come to Me and drink. He who believes in Me, as the Scripture has said, out of his heart will flow rivers of living water."

Miracle Evangelism

As God's divine love continues to flow from us, we will be moving in His power and compassion. We will continue to reach out in miracle evangelism to the lost of this world.

Sacrifice of Praise

The sacrifice of praise is offered to God when things don't seem to go right.

It is:

➢ Praise offered in spite of the way things are going
➢ Praise offered in faith and obedience
➢ Praise offered because of who God is

Hebrews 13:15 Therefore by Him let us continually offer the sacrifice of praise to God, that is, the fruit of our lips, giving thanks to His name.

As we reach out in miracle evangelism, Satan and his demons will try to bring all types of obstacles, problems, and fear of failure against us. It's at this time, we must continue to offer the sacrifice of praise.

➢ *Paul and Silas*

Paul and Silas are powerful examples of how we are to give the sacrifice of praise.

Acts 16:22-26 Then the multitude rose up together against them; and the magistrates tore off their clothes and commanded them to be beaten with rods. And when they had laid many stripes on them, they threw them into prison, commanding the jailer to keep them securely. Having received such a charge, he put them into the inner prison and fastened their feet in the stocks.

But at midnight Paul and Silas were praying and singing hymns to God, and the prisoners were listening to them. Suddenly there was a great earthquake, so that the foundations of the prison were shaken; and immediately all the doors were opened and everyone's chains were loosed.

Psalms 34:1 I will bless the Lord at all times; His praise shall continually be in my mouth.

The sacrifice of praise is a continual and audible praise. This scripture shows that the sacrifice of praise offered to God in adverse circumstances causes the divine intervention of God in our lives, family, church, nation and the world.

Praise Brings Victory

➢ *King Jehoshaphat's Victory*

When King Jehoshaphat and the people of Israel were faced with a powerful enemy, the king and the people began to praise the Lord. The emphasis wasn't on how powerful the enemy was. They praised the God who ruled over all the nations. Then God spoke to them and promised them the victory.

Jehoshaphat spoke:
2 Chronicles 20:6-9 "O Lord God of our fathers, are You not God in heaven, and do You not rule over all the kingdoms of the nations, and in Your hand is there not power and might, so that no one is able to withstand You?

"Are You not our God, who drove out the inhabitants of this land before Your people Israel, and gave it to the descendants of Abraham Your friend forever? And they dwell in it, and have built You a sanctuary in it for Your name, saying, If disaster comes upon us, such as the sword, judgment, pestilence, or famine, we will stand before this temple and in Your presence (for Your name is in this temple), and cry out to You in our affliction, and You will hear and save."

The spirit of the Lord came up on Jahaziel:

Vs. 15-18 ... and he said, "Listen, all you of Judah and you inhabitants of Jerusalem, and you, King Jehoshaphat! Thus says the Lord to you: 'Do not be afraid nor dismayed because of this great multitude, for the battle is not yours, but God's. Tomorrow go down against them. They will surely come up by the ascent of Ziz, and you will find them at the end of the brook before the Wilderness of Jeruel. You will not need to fight in this battle. Position yourselves, stand still and see the salvation of the Lord, who is with you, O Judah and Jerusalem!' Do not fear or be dismayed; tomorrow go out against them, for the Lord is with you."

And Jehoshaphat bowed his head with his face to the ground, and all Judah and the inhabitants of Jerusalem bowed before the Lord, worshiping the Lord.

➤ *Believers Today*

As we begin to praise and worship the Lord, He sets ambushes against the enemy. Jehoshaphat and the children of Israel began to offer praise, not after the enemy was defeated, but while the enemy was still surrounding them and their situation seemed hopeless.

2 Chronicles 20:20-24 And they rose early in the morning and went out into the Wilderness of Tekoa; and as they went out, Jehoshaphat stood and said, "Hear me, O Judah and you inhabitants of Jerusalem: believe in the Lord your God, and you shall be established; believe His prophets, and you shall prosper."

And when he had consulted with the people, he appointed those who should sing to the Lord, and who should praise the beauty of holiness, as they went out before the army and were saying: "Praise the Lord, for His mercy endures forever."

Now when they began to sing and to praise, the Lord set ambushes against the people of Ammon, Moab, and Mount Seir, who had come against Judah; and they were defeated.

> For the people of Ammon and Moab stood up against the inhabitants of Mount Seir to utterly kill and destroy them. And when they had made an end of the inhabitants of Seir, they helped to destroy one another.
>
> So when Judah came to a place overlooking the wilderness, they looked toward the multitude; and there were their dead bodies, fallen on the earth. No one had escaped.

Today, we too can take our cities and the nations of the world through praise. The power of God is released when we praise Him. Angels move into action on our behalf. We too will see great victories won through miracle evangelism. We too will experience great joy.

> 2 Chronicles 20:27-29 Then they returned, every man of Judah and Jerusalem, with Jehoshaphat in front of them, to go back to Jerusalem with joy, for the Lord had made them rejoice over their enemies. So they came to Jerusalem, with stringed instruments and harps and trumpets, to the house of the Lord. And the fear of God was on all the kingdoms of those countries when they heard that the Lord had fought against the enemies of Israel.

In miracle evangelism, as we go into homes, cities, and nations with praises, God will act on our behalf against our enemies. We will see hearts prepared and doors open for people to receive Jesus. We will take our cities for God!

QUESTIONS FOR REVIEW

1. What are the two prerequisites to releasing the global harvest?

2. List seven characteristics of effective prayer for releasing the global harvest.

3. Give a biblical example of victory that came as a result of praise to God.

Lesson Seven

The Army of God

AN EXCEEDING GREAT ARMY

The prophet Ezekiel prophesied about a valley of dry bones. He was prophesying concerning the nation of Israel. But when we look around at the church of our day, we are surrounded by the discouraged, wounded, helpless wrecks of what were once beautiful, vibrant, active Christians.

This is not the type of army God describes. He speaks of an authoritative, forceful army which will powerfully advance the kingdom of God.

The breath of the Holy Spirit is restoring the army of God for a world-wide harvest of souls.

We can believe with Ezekiel:

Ezekiel 37:10 So I prophesied as He commanded me, and breath came into them, and they lived, and stood upon their feet, an exceedingly great army.

Gideon, an Example

The army which God is raising up today is not dependent on great numbers. It's dependent on the power of God. When the nation of Israel was under the domination of the cruel Midianites, God sent an angel to one man, Gideon.

Judges 6:12 And the Angel of the Lord appeared to him, and said to him, "The Lord is with you, you mighty man of valor!"

God spoke. Gideon believed and acted on that word. Notice that God did not need a large number of men. He needed dedicated men who were alert and not afraid.

Judges 7:1-7 Then Jerubbaal (that is, Gideon) and all the people who were with him rose early and encamped beside the well of Harod ...

And the Lord said to Gideon, "The people who are with you are too many for Me to give the Midianites into their hands, lest Israel claim glory for itself against Me, saying, 'My own hand has saved me.'

"Now therefore, proclaim in the hearing of the people, saying, 'Whoever is fearful and afraid, let him turn and depart at once from Mount Gilead.'" And twenty-two thousand of the people returned, and ten thousand remained.

And the Lord said to Gideon, "The people are still too many; bring them down to the water, and I will test them for you there. Then it will be, that of whom I say to you, 'This one shall go with you,' the

same shall go with you; and of whomever I say to you, 'This one shall not go with you,' the same shall not go."

So he brought the people down to the water. And the Lord said to Gideon, "Everyone who laps from the water with his tongue, as a dog laps, you shall set apart by himself; likewise everyone who gets down on his knees to drink."

And the number of those who lapped, putting their hand to their mouth, was three hundred men; but all the rest of the people got down on their knees to drink water.

Then the Lord said to Gideon, "By the three hundred men who lapped I will save you, and deliver the Midianites into your hand. Let all the other people go, every man to his place."

God is drawing men and women all over the world to prepare for and engage in battle. We are to be a mighty army going forth in the power of His Spirit and His word, like mighty warriors invading the forces of the enemy, regaining the territory lost to the enemy.

God is speaking to the church of our day just as He spoke to Gideon, "The Lord is with you, you mighty man of valor".

Joel's Prophecy
➤ *Prepare for War!*

The battle cry which went forth from the prophet Joel is still going forth today. It's still the battle cry of the Lord to His servants all over the world.

Joel 2:1,11;3:9 Blow the trumpet in Zion, and sound an alarm in My holy mountain! Let all the inhabitants of the land tremble; for the day of the Lord is coming, for it is at hand.

The Lord gives voice before His army, for His camp is very great; for strong is the One who executes His word. For the day of the Lord is great and very terrible; who can endure it?

Proclaim this among the nations: "Prepare for war! Wake up the mighty men, let all the men of war draw near, let them come up."

There is awakening in the hearts of believers, a strong desire to be mighty men and women for God.

➤ *Forceful Advance*

It's an aggressive army which goes forth in aggressive compassion, aggressive faith, and aggressive obedience to forcibly advance the kingdom of God.

Matthew 11:12 "And from the days of John the Baptist until now the kingdom of heaven suffers violence, and the violent take it by force."

Global Harvest

The purpose of the gathering of the army of God is global harvest. The end-time is near. Jesus is coming soon. The Spirit of God is moving all over the world with signs, wonders and creative miracles such as never heard or seen before.

Joel's prophecy continued.

Joel 3:13,14 Put in the sickle, for the harvest is ripe. Come, go down; for the winepress is full, the vats overflow–for their wickedness is great.

Multitudes, multitudes in the valley of decision! For the day of the Lord is near in the valley of decision.

THE ARMOR OF GOD

God has certainly not left us defenseless against the enemy. He has provided armor for our protection and victory.

Ephesians 6:10-17 Finally, my brethren, be strong in the Lord and in the power of His might. Put on the whole armor of God, that you may be able to stand against the wiles of the devil. For we do not wrestle against flesh and blood, but against principalities, against powers, against the rulers of the darkness of this age, against spiritual hosts of wickedness in the heavenly places.

Therefore take up the whole armor of God, that you may be able to withstand in the evil day, and having done all, to stand. Stand therefore, having girded your waist with truth, having put on the breastplate of righteousness, and having shod your feet with the preparation of the gospel of peace; above all, taking the shield of faith with which you will be able to quench all the fiery darts of the wicked one. And take the helmet of salvation, and the sword of the Spirit, which is the word of God.

We must learn to put on the whole armor of God before we face the enemy. It's time to get prepared, to get armed with our spiritual weapons, to get protected by the covering of the blood and the shield of faith.

Truth

Truth is like a belt, it holds everything in place. Without integrity in our personal life, none of God's armor will fit.

Righteousness

Righteousness provides protection from the enemy. When we are covered with the breastplate of righteousness, we will be able to stand against the attacks of the enemy.

Gospel of Peace

The gospel of peace provides stability and security so we will be able to stand firm against the enemy.

Shield of Faith

The shield of faith provides overall protection. It will quench the fiery darts of the enemy.

Helmet of Salvation

The helmet of salvation protects the head. When we understand the total salvation God has provided for mankind and renew our minds with that salvation, we will be protected.

Sword of the Spirit

The sword of the Spirit is the only offensive weapon we have. It's the word of God. Satan has no defense which can stop this powerful weapon when we believe and speak the word of God from our mouths. We can use the sword of the Spirit to forcibly advance the kingdom of God.

Praying in Tongues

Prayer allows the power of God to flow through our lives. When we are fully armed for battle only then through prayer do we enter the battleground.

If we are not prayer warriors, we are not fighting in the Lord's army.

Ephesians 6:18 ... praying always with all prayer and supplication in the Spirit, being watchful to this end with all perseverance and supplication for all the saints ...

THE KEYS OF THE KINGDOM

Jesus took back the keys to the kingdom and He has given them to us. The church has the responsibility to use these keys to bring the gospel to the nations of the world.

Revelation 1:18 "I am He who lives, and was dead, and behold, I am alive forevermore. Amen. And I have the keys of Hades and of Death."

Matthew 16:19 "And I will give you the keys of the kingdom of heaven, and whatever you bind on earth will be bound in heaven, and whatever you loose on earth will be loosed in heaven."

Blood of Jesus

The first key to victory we have is the blood of Jesus. At the moment we accept Jesus as our Lord and Savior this key became available to us.

Hebrews 9:12,14 Not with the blood of goats and calves, but with His own blood He entered the Most Holy Place once for all, having obtained eternal redemption. For if the blood of bulls and goats and the ashes of a heifer, sprinkling the unclean, sanctifies for the purifying of the flesh, how much more shall the blood of Christ, who through the eternal Spirit offered Himself without spot to God, purge your conscience from dead works to serve the living God?

- *Overcome Through Blood*

By the blood of Jesus, we are restored to the original position which Adam lost to Satan. We are no longer hopeless and defeated. We are once again victorious overcomers.

We can overcome Satan through the blood of Jesus.

Revelation 12:11 "And they overcame him by the blood of the Lamb and by the word of their testimony, and they did not love their lives to the death."

- *Protection Through Blood*

There is protection and victory through the blood. We should start boldly confessing that we are covered with the blood of Jesus and that we overcome Satan by the blood of the Lamb.

Word of God

When the word of God is spoken from our mouth, it becomes a powerful force in our lives. The word of God is our sword of the spirit.

- *Word Brings Victory*

The apostle John wrote of young men who knew the word of God and thus had the victory.

1 John 2:14b I have written to you, young men, because you are strong, and the word of God abides in you, and you have overcome the wicked one.

When we know and speak the word of God, we can have the victory.

- *Speak the Word*

The centurion who came to Jesus for healing for his servant understood authority and the importance of the spoken word.

Matthew 8:8-10 The centurion answered and said, "Lord, I am not worthy that You should come under my roof. But only speak a word, and my servant will be healed. For I also am a man under authority, having soldiers under me. And I say to this one, 'Go,' and he goes; and to another, 'Come,' and he comes; and to my servant, 'Do this,' and he does it."

When Jesus heard it, He marveled, and said to those who followed, "Assuredly, I say to you, I have not found such great faith, not even in Israel!"

Name of Jesus

Jesus promised that when those who believed in His name went into all the world and preached His gospel, signs and wonders would follow.

Mark 16:15-18 And He said to them, "Go into all the world and preach the gospel to every creature. He who believes and is baptized will be saved; but he who does not believe will be condemned.

"And these signs will follow those who believe: in My name they will cast out demons; they will speak with new tongues; they will take up serpents; and if they drink anything deadly, it will by no means hurt them; they will lay hands on the sick, and they will recover."

➤ *Ask in His Name*

Jesus gave us the right and the privilege to use His name. He instructed us to use His name.

John 14:12-14 "Most assuredly, I say to you, he who believes in Me, the works that I do he will do also; and greater works than these he will do, because I go to My Father. And whatever you ask in My name, that I will do, that the Father may be glorified in the Son."

John 16:23,24 "And in that day you will ask Me nothing. Most assuredly, I say to you, whatever you ask the Father in My name He will give you. Until now you have asked nothing in My name. Ask, and you will receive, that your joy may be full."

➤ *Above Every Name*

The name of Jesus is above every other name. At His name every knee should bow both in the heavenly realm and in the natural realm.

Philippians 2:9,10 Therefore God also has highly exalted Him and given Him the name which is above every name, that at the name of Jesus every knee should bow, of those in heaven, and of those on earth, and of those under the earth.

➤ *Healing in Name*

Peter and John brought healing in the name of Jesus.

Acts 3:6,12,16 Then Peter said, "Silver and gold I do not have, but what I do have I give you: in the name of Jesus Christ of Nazareth, rise up and walk."

So when Peter saw it, he responded to the people: "Men of Israel, why do you marvel at this? Or why look so intently at us, as though by our own power or godliness we had made this man walk?

"And His name, through faith in His name, has made this man strong, whom you see and know. Yes, the faith which comes through Him has given him this perfect soundness in the presence of you all."

➤ *Demons Submit*

Paul commanded the demons to leave in the name of Jesus.

Acts 16:18 And this she did for many days. But Paul, greatly annoyed, turned and said to the spirit, "I command you in the name of Jesus Christ to come out of her." And he came out that very hour.

Summary

Every believer who is in the Great Commission Army must be able to operate the three keys in miracle evangelism. In the book of Acts, we see how the disciples used these keys to bring in a great harvest of souls.

Today, as in the book of Acts, a mighty army of God is arising, armed with these powerful keys of victory. Signs and wonders are confirming God's word in the streets of our cities. Armed and equipped for miracle evangelism, the army of God has begun the great end-time harvest.

QUESTIONS FOR REVIEW

1. Who is in God's army today?

2. Name the parts of the armor and what is the use of each.

3. What are the three keys of miracle evangelism?

Lesson Eight

Power Evangelism in Action

The clergy-laymen tradition has been broken. God is raising up a new breed of believers. They are bold to enter in and do the same works Jesus did.

POWER EVANGELISTS

Harvest Field

Jesus said the harvest was plentiful but the workers were few. Our Father-God is the Lord of the Harvest, and He has sent workers into the field.

Matthew 9:37,38 Then He said to His disciples, "The harvest truly is plentiful, but the laborers are few. Therefore pray the Lord of the harvest to send out laborers into His harvest."

Law of Sowing – Reaping

God's law of sowing and reaping is still in effect.

The church will reap what she sows in every area. If we don't give up, we will see the harvest.

Galatians 6:7-9 Do not be deceived, God is not mocked; for whatever a man sows, that he will also reap. For he who sows to his flesh will of the flesh reap corruption, but he who sows to the Spirit will of the Spirit reap everlasting life. And let us not grow weary while doing good, for in due season we shall reap if we do not lose heart.

Supply – Increase

God has promised to supply both the seed for sowing and the bread for provisions. He has even promised to multiply the seed and to increase our fruit.

2 Corinthians 9:10 Now may He who supplies seed to the sower, and bread for food, supply and multiply the seed you have sown and increase the fruits of your righteousness.

Miracle Evangelism

Miracles were an important part of Jesus' instructions for evangelism in the Great Commission.

Mark 16:15,17,18,20 And He said to them, "Go into all the world and preach the gospel to every creature. And these signs will follow those who believe: in My name they will cast out demons; they will speak with new tongues; they will take up serpents; and if they drink anything deadly, it will by no means hurt them; they will lay hands on the sick, and they will recover."

And they went out and preached everywhere, the Lord working with them and confirming the word through the accompanying signs. Amen.

Matthew 28:19,20 "Go therefore and make disciples of all the nations, baptizing them in the name of the Father and of the Son and of the Holy Spirit, teaching them to observe all things that I have commanded you; and lo, I am with you always, even to the end of the age." Amen.

Jesus said we are to go into all the world and make disciples of all nations. We are to baptize and teach them to do everything Jesus has commanded. We are to teach believers how to be effective in evangelism, how to cast out demons, and lay hands on the sick.

Jesus, Our Example

Jesus began His ministry by personally:

- teaching
- preaching
- healing
- bringing deliverance and recovery
- setting captives free
- having compassion

Luke 4:18 "The Spirit of the Lord is upon Me, because He has anointed Me to preach the gospel to the poor. He has sent Me to heal the brokenhearted, to preach deliverance to the captives and recovery of sight to the blind, to set at liberty those who are oppressed."

Matthew 9:35,36 And Jesus went about all the cities and villages, teaching in their synagogues, preaching the gospel of the kingdom, and healing every sickness and every disease among the people. But when He saw the multitudes, He was moved with compassion for them, because they were weary and scattered, like sheep having no shepherd.

John 14:12 "Most assuredly, I say to you, he who believes in Me, the works that I do he will do also; and greater works than these he will do, because I go to My Father."

MULTIPLICATION

At first, the ministry of Jesus was limited to one village or city at a time.

Twelve Disciples

Then Jesus began to multiply His ministry by commissioning the twelve disciples. They were to do the same ministry He had been demonstrating to them. They were to operate with the same love and compassion Jesus had.

Matthew 9:36-38 But when He saw the multitudes, He was moved with compassion for them, because they were weary and scattered, like sheep having no shepherd.

Then He said to His disciples, "The harvest truly is plentiful, but the laborers are few. Therefore pray the Lord of the harvest to send out laborers into His harvest."

Twelve Disciples

First the disciples were instructed to pray for the harvest. Then they were commissioned – given power – and sent out.

Matthew 10:1,5a,7,8 And when He had called His twelve disciples to Him, He gave them power over unclean spirits, to cast them out, and to heal all kinds of sickness and all kinds of disease.

These twelve Jesus sent out and commanded them, saying "... as you go, preach, saying, 'The kingdom of heaven is at hand.' Heal the sick, cleanse the lepers, raise the dead, cast out demons. Freely you have received, freely give."

Seventy Disciples

After the twelve disciples had returned rejoicing, Jesus commissioned seventy more disciples and sent them out.

Luke 10:1,9 After these things the Lord appointed seventy others also, and sent them two by two before His face into every city and place where He Himself was about to go. And heal the sick who are there, and say to them, 'The kingdom of God has come near to you.'

Every Believer

Just before Jesus left this earth, He commissioned all believers and sent them out. The believers are to do the works of Jesus and even greater works than Jesus.

Mark 16:15,17,18 And He said to them, "Go into all the world and preach the gospel to every creature. And these signs will follow those who believe: in My name they will cast out demons; they will speak with new tongues; they will take up serpents; and if they drink anything deadly, it will by no means hurt them; they will lay hands on the sick, and they will recover."

Jesus said when we proclaim the gospel, He would be with us confirming His word by miracles. We should expect miracles.

Jesus instructed us to do exactly the same works He did on this earth. To know God's pattern for effective evangelism, we should read Matthew, Mark, Luke and John and picture ourselves doing exactly the same works as Jesus did.

John 14:12 "Most assuredly, I say to you, he who believes in Me, the works that I do he will do also; and greater works than these he will do, because I go to My Father."

The works of Jesus are not finished. John said that if all His deeds were written in books even the world could not hold them.

John 21:25 And there are also many other things that Jesus did, which if they were written one by one, I suppose that even the world itself could not contain the books that would be written. Amen.

Same Power

The same power, the Holy Spirit who came on Jesus to equip Him for His earthly ministry, is available to empower believers today.

Acts 1:8 But you shall receive power when the Holy Spirit has come upon you; and you shall be witnesses to Me in Jerusalem, and in all Judea and Samaria, and to the end of the earth.

The power which comes through the baptism in the Holy Spirit, is the power to be a witness for Jesus Christ. The power of God is provided for every believer to be effective in miracle evangelism.

POWER EVANGELISM

Supernatural Encounters

Pagan religions often demonstrate supernatural manifestations by the power of demons. To reach the lost who are bound by these demonic religions, it's necessary that believers, who are full of the Spirit of God, demonstrate His greater power through signs and wonders. The working of miracles, signs and wonders are the power tools God has given to His body.

T.L. Osborn has written,

It is 'this gospel of the kingdom', preached in the power of the Holy Spirit, confirmed by signs and wonders and divers miracles, that always produces the greatest evangelistic triumph in any generation.

The vast majority of the people of this world has a supernatural orientation. They want, need and will accept only a gospel which comes with supernatural power – a power stronger than their own.

A power encounter is a visible, practical demonstration that Jesus Christ is more powerful than the false gods and spirits they worship and fear.

John Wimber has written in his book, *Power Evangelism*,

Any system or force that must be overcome for the gospel to be believed is cause for a power encounter.

The writer of the book of Hebrews wrote of the importance of signs, wonders, miracles, and the gifts of the Holy Spirit in reaching the lost.

Hebrews 2:3,4 ... how shall we escape if we neglect so great a salvation, which at the first began to be spoken by the Lord, and was confirmed to us by those who heard Him, God also bearing witness both with signs and wonders, with various miracles, and gifts of the Holy Spirit, according to His own will?

Miracles in Evidence

A gospel which is confirmed by signs and wonders will produce tremendous results. Whether it was Peter, Philip or Paul the same results always followed:

➢ they proclaimed the gospel
➢ miracles were in evidence
➢ multitudes believed

Paul said the gospel was the power of God.

Romans 1:16 For I am not ashamed of the gospel of Christ, for it is the power of God to salvation for everyone who believes, for the Jew first and also for the Greek.

Miracles always accompanied the preaching of the word.

Mark 16:20 And they went out and preached everywhere, the Lord working with them and confirming the word through the accompanying signs. Amen.

When signs and wonders confirm the proclamation of the gospel, people always come to Jesus.

As we study Acts, we discover that each time people were filled with the Holy Spirit, they became powerful miracle-working evangelists for Jesus Christ.

Power of Jesus

Jesus said He was anointed by the Holy Spirit to preach.

Luke 4:18 "The Spirit of the Lord is upon Me, because He has anointed Me to preach the gospel to the poor. He has sent Me to heal the brokenhearted, to preach deliverance to the captives and recovery of sight to the blind, to set at liberty those who are oppressed."

Preaching without the anointing of the Holy Spirit is ineffective. Powerful anointed preaching always produces results.

New Testament Pattern
➢ *Philip at Samaria*

Philip provided a New Testament pattern for miracle evangelism.

Acts 8:5-8 Then Philip went down to the city of Samaria and preached Christ to them. And the multitudes with one accord heeded the things spoken by Philip, hearing and seeing the miracles which he did. For unclean spirits, crying with a loud voice, came out of many who were possessed; and many who were paralyzed and lame were healed. And there was great joy in that city.

Miracle Evangelism

The people in Samaria heard the things spoken by Philip, and saw the miracles that he did.

> *Philip and Ethiopian*

Philip wasn't only obedient and faithful in mass evangelism, he was obedient and effective in personal evangelism.

Acts 8:26-31 Now an angel of the Lord spoke to Philip, saying, "Arise and go toward the south along the road which goes down from Jerusalem to Gaza." This is desert.

So he arose and went. And behold, a man of Ethiopia, a eunuch of great authority under Candace the queen of the Ethiopians, who had charge of all her treasury, and had come to Jerusalem to worship, was returning. And sitting in his chariot, he was reading Isaiah the prophet.

Then the Spirit said to Philip, "Go near and overtake this chariot."

So Philip ran to him, and heard him reading the prophet Isaiah, and said, "Do you understand what you are reading?"

And he said, "How can I, unless someone guides me?" And he asked Philip to come up and sit with him.

It says that Philip "preached" Jesus to him.

Acts 8:35 Then Philip opened his mouth, and beginning at this Scripture, preached Jesus to him.

When many people hear the Great Commission, they exclaim, "I can't preach! I could never stand before a large group of people and talk! Certainly, Jesus wasn't talking to people like me! He must have been speaking to those He has called to be preachers!"

Mark 16:15 And He said to them, "Go into all the world and preach the gospel to every creature."

Mark continued:
Mark 16:17a "And these signs will follow those who believe ..."

All believers are to preach the gospel. However, preaching doesn't mean that we must stand behind a pulpit, and preach to a group of people. In the example of Philip and the Ethiopian, we see Philip sitting and preaching to him on a one-to-one basis.

"To preach" means to proclaim or simply to share the gospel of Jesus Christ everywhere we go.

Acts 8:36-38 Now as they went down the road, they came to some water. And the eunuch said, "See, here is water. What hinders me from being baptized?"

Then Philip said, "If you believe with all your heart, you may." And he answered and said, "I believe that Jesus Christ is the Son of God."

So he commanded the chariot to stand still. And both Philip and the eunuch went down into the water, and he baptized him.

> *Paul's Strategy*

Paul said he had "fully preached" the gospel.

Romans 15:18-21 For I will not dare to speak of any of those things which Christ has not accomplished through me, in word and deed, to make the Gentiles obedient–in mighty signs and wonders, by the power of the Spirit of God, so that from Jerusalem and round about to Illyricum I have fully preached the gospel of Christ.

And so I have made it my aim to preach the gospel, not where Christ was named, lest I should build on another man's foundation, but as it is written: "To whom He was not announced, they shall see; and those who have not heard shall understand."

Paul was committed to frontier miracle evangelism. Notice that the people who had never heard, saw and understood. What did they see? The mighty signs and wonders.

There are three avenues of evangelism:

> word
> deed
> signs and wonders

A careful, Spirit-orchestrated mix of God's word, deeds and miracles is the Bible's strategy for reaching the nations for the Lord Jesus.

1 Corinthians 2:1-5 And I, brethren, when I came to you, did not come with excellence of speech or of wisdom declaring to you the testimony of God. For I determined not to know anything among you except Jesus Christ and Him crucified. I was with you in weakness, in fear, and in much trembling. And my speech and my preaching were not with persuasive words of human wisdom, but in demonstration of the Spirit and of power, that your faith should not be in the wisdom of men but in the power of God.

Militant Christianity

To be effective evangelists in any culture, we must be convinced of four truths. They are:

> power in the gospel
> power in God's word
> power in the name of Jesus
> evangelism must be done in power

Christianity in the book of Acts was expanded by aggressive, militant power evangelism.

Our warfare is not with flesh and blood, or with human beings, but with the forces of darkness.

Miracle Evangelism

The kingdom of God is extended by forcibly advancing against the kingdoms Satan has established on this earth. Effective evangelism includes aggressive spiritual warfare and a demonstration of the power of God through miracle evangelism.

Matthew 11:12 "And from the days of John the Baptist until now the kingdom of heaven suffers violence, and the violent take it by force."

QUESTIONS FOR REVIEW

1. What is a power encounter and when is it necessary?

2. Why did the multitudes in Samaria give heed to Philip's preaching?

3. What four truths must we be convinced of to be an effective evangelist in any culture?

Lesson Nine

Ministering by the Anointing

The anointing is the tangible presence of God. It's the impartation of His ability on an available, yielded vessel to carry out His will and work. Learning to flow with what God is doing is the key to setting others free. The anointing can be stored, transferred and imparted through the laying on of hands.

We will study how Jesus needed the anointing of the Holy Spirit. All that Jesus did in His earthly ministry was by the anointing and the gifts of the Holy Spirit. He heard and saw into the spirit realm by the revelation gifts before He moved in the vocal and power gifts. Therefore, anyone who wants to do the same works that Jesus did must learn how to minister by the anointing.

The primary way God leads His people is by the anointing of the Holy Spirit. All visions, revelations, impressions and manifestations must be checked by the anointing within. In miracle evangelism, all impressions must receive the confirmation of our own inner witness. As we step out and operate in the vocal and power gifts, we will see miracles take place and people respond to the gospel.

The world cannot be evangelized without the power and anointing of the Holy Spirit.

PROMISE OF HOLY SPIRIT

Promised in Old Testament

The anointing of the Holy Spirit was promised in the Old Testament.

Joel 2:28,29 "And it shall come to pass afterward that I will pour out My Spirit on all flesh; your sons and your daughters shall prophesy, your old men shall dream dreams, your young men shall see visions; and also on My menservants and on My maidservants I will pour out My Spirit in those days."

Promised in New Testament

The filling of the Holy Spirit was promised in the New Testament.

Luke 24:49 "Behold, I send the Promise of My Father upon you; but tarry in the city of Jerusalem until you are endued with power from on high."

John 7:37-39 On the last day, that great day of the feast, Jesus stood and cried out, saying, "If anyone thirsts, let him come to Me and drink. He who believes in Me, as the Scripture has said, out of his heart will flow rivers of living water."

Miracle Evangelism

But this He spoke concerning the Spirit, whom those believing in Him would receive; for the Holy Spirit was not yet given, because Jesus was not yet glorified.

Acts 2:38,39 Then Peter said to them, "Repent, and let every one of you be baptized in the name of Jesus Christ for the remission of sins; and you shall receive the gift of the Holy Spirit. For the promise is to you and to your children, and to all who are afar off, as many as the Lord our God will call."

Promise Received

On the day of Pentecost, the Holy Spirit came just as Jesus had promised.

Acts 2:1-4 Now when the Day of Pentecost had fully come, they were all with one accord in one place. And suddenly there came a sound from heaven, as of a rushing mighty wind, and it filled the whole house where they were sitting. Then there appeared to them divided tongues, as of fire, and one sat upon each of them. And they were all filled with the Holy Spirit and began to speak with other tongues, as the Spirit gave them utterance.

To receive the gift of the Holy Spirit, we are to simply ask for it and receive it by faith.

Luke 11:11-13 If a son asks for bread from any father among you, will he give him a stone? Or if he asks for a fish, will he give him a serpent instead of a fish? Or if he asks for an egg, will he offer him a scorpion? If you then, being evil, know how to give good gifts to your children, how much more will your heavenly Father give the Holy Spirit to those who ask Him!

The filling with the Holy Spirit is a good gift from the Father. He desires to give it to you.

Jesus, Our Example

Jesus operated as a man when He was on the earth. The word says God anointed Him with the Holy Spirit and power.

Acts 10:38 ... how God anointed Jesus of Nazareth with the Holy Spirit and with power, who went about doing good and healing all who were oppressed by the devil, for God was with Him.

Luke 3:21,22 Now when all the people were baptized, it came to pass that Jesus also was baptized; and while He prayed, the heaven was opened. And the Holy Spirit descended in bodily form like a dove upon Him, and a voice came from heaven which said, "You are My beloved Son; in You I am well pleased."

Jesus said He was anointed to preach the gospel.

Luke 4:18 "The Spirit of the Lord is upon Me, because He has anointed Me to preach the gospel to the poor. He has sent Me to heal the brokenhearted, to preach deliverance to the captives and recovery of sight to the blind, to set at liberty those who are oppressed."

If Jesus had ministered as the Son of God, He would not have needed the anointing of the Holy Spirit. However, He ministered as the Last Adam, as a man, as God manifested in the flesh, and He operated through the anointing of the Holy Spirit just as believers are to do today.

THE ANOINTING

Same as Jesus

To do the works Jesus did, we need the same anointing which was on Him. Jesus was speaking to all believers who are to do His works. He wasn't speaking to just the apostles, or to just those of the fivefold ministry. He qualifies all believers to receive the same anointing to do His works.

John 14:12 "Most assuredly, I say to you, he who believes in Me, the works that I do he will do also; and greater works than these he will do, because I go to My Father."

Anointing Within

Every believer has an anointing within which comes with the indwelling presence of the Holy Spirit. In addition to this, God gives a special anointing to believers when He selects them for specific tasks or ministries.

The anointing on a believer's life functions in the realm of the Spirit by the operation of the supernatural gifts of the Holy Spirit.

1 John 2:27 But the anointing which you have received from Him abides in you, and you do not need that anyone teach you; but as the same anointing teaches you concerning all things, and is true, and is not a lie, and just as it has taught you, you will abide in Him.

In the Old Testament, believers didn't have the abiding presence of the Holy Spirit within them as we have since the day of Pentecost. Instead, the Holy Spirit would come on a prophet, a priest, or a king to empower them to perform certain functions.

1 Samuel 10:6,7 Then the Spirit of the LORD will come upon you, and you will prophesy with them and be turned into another man. And let it Be, when these signs come to You, that you do as the occasion demands: for God is with you.

REASONS FOR ANOINTING

Works of Jesus

The anointing of the Holy Spirit is necessary if we are to do the works which Jesus did.

Mark 16:17,18 "And these signs will follow those who believe: in My name they will cast out demons; they will speak with new tongues; they will take up serpents; and if they drink anything deadly, it will by no means hurt them; they will lay hands on the sick, and they will recover."

Matthew 28:16-20 Then the eleven disciples went away into Galilee, to the mountain which Jesus had appointed for them. And when they saw Him, they worshiped Him; but some doubted.

Then Jesus came and spoke to them, saying, "All authority has been given to Me in heaven and on earth. Go therefore and make disciples of all the nations, baptizing them in the name of the Father and of the Son and of the Holy Spirit, teaching them to observe all things that I have commanded you; and lo, I am with you always, even to the end of the age." Amen.

Bearing Fruit

It's through the anointing of the Holy Spirit that believers can bear good fruit.

John 15:7,8,16 "If you abide in Me, and My words abide in you, you will ask what you desire, and it shall be done for you. By this My Father is glorified, that you bear much fruit; so you will be My disciples. You did not choose Me, but I chose you and appointed you that you should go and bear fruit, and that your fruit should remain, that whatever you ask the Father in My name He may give you."

Being Reconciled

Through Jesus Christ, we have been reconciled to God. Now we are to reconcile the world to God.

2 Corinthians 5:17-21 Therefore, if anyone is in Christ, he is a new creation; old things have passed away; behold, all things have become new. Now all things are of God, who has reconciled us to Himself through Jesus Christ, and has given us the ministry of reconciliation, that is, that God was in Christ reconciling the world to Himself, not imputing their trespasses to them, and has committed to us the word of reconciliation.

Therefore we are ambassadors for Christ, as though God were pleading through us: we implore you on Christ's behalf, be reconciled to God. For He made Him who knew no sin to be sin for us, that we might become the righteousness of God in Him.

Fashioned after Christ

We are to be fashioned and shaped after Christ.

2 Corinthians 3:18 But we all, with unveiled face, beholding as in a mirror the glory of the Lord, are being transformed into the same image from glory to glory, just as by the Spirit of the Lord.

Teaching

The anointing of God will teach and confirm all things.

1 John 2:20,27 But you have an anointing from the Holy One, and you know all things.

But the anointing which you have received from Him abides in you, and you do not need that anyone teach you; but as the same anointing teaches you concerning all things, and is true, and is not a lie, and just as it has taught you, you will abide in Him.

Recognizing Calling

We must learn to wait for the Holy Spirit to move and to recognize the function God called us to.

Acts 10:38 "... how God anointed Jesus of Nazareth with the Holy Spirit and with power, who went about doing good and healing all who were oppressed by the devil, for God was with Him."

We must believe that God's Spirit is on us.

People need to see, believe and respect the anointing.

Matthew 20:30-34 And behold, two blind men sitting by the road, when they heard that Jesus was passing by, cried out, saying, "Have mercy on us, O Lord, Son of David!"

Then the multitude warned them that they should be quiet; but they cried out all the more, saying, "Have mercy on us, O Lord, Son of David!"

So Jesus stood still and called them, and said, "What do you want Me to do for you?"

They said to Him, "Lord, that our eyes may be opened."

So Jesus had compassion and touched their eyes. And immediately their eyes received sight, and they followed Him.

The multitudes saw the anointing that was on Jesus. They saw the blind men, and tried to quiet them. Then they saw the anointing in action as the blind men received their sight.

Learning to Minister

When we learn to flow with the Holy Spirit there will be:

- Awareness
- Sensitivity
- Availability

- ➢ Positive thoughts
- ➢ Obedience

We will:

- ➢ Understand
- ➢ Cooperate with
- ➢ Work under leading of Spirit

We must learn to be led by the Spirit. Learning to flow with what God is doing, is the key to effective ministry.

Romans 8:14 For as many as are led by the Spirit of God, these are sons of God.

Proverbs 20:27 The spirit of a man is the lamp of the Lord, searching all the inner depths of his heart.

Inward Witness

When we are operating in the anointing of the Holy Spirit there will be an inner witness with our spirits.

Romans 8:16 The Spirit Himself bears witness with our spirit that we are children of God ...

John 14:20 "At that day you will know that I am in My Father, and you in Me, and I in you."

Inward Voice

Our conscience is the voice or witness of the Holy Spirit within.

Romans 9:1 I tell the truth in Christ, I am not lying, my conscience also bearing me witness in the Holy Spirit.

1 John 3:20,21 For if our heart condemns us, God is greater than our heart, and knows all things. Beloved, if our heart does not condemn us, we have confidence toward God.

Obedience

When we hear God through the revelation gifts of the Holy Spirit and obey Him, we will be as effective as Philip was.

Acts 8:26-31 Now an angel of the Lord spoke to Philip, saying, "Arise and go toward the south along the road which goes down from Jerusalem to Gaza." This is desert. So he arose and went. And behold, a man of Ethiopia, a eunuch of great authority under Candace the queen of the Ethiopians, who had charge of all her treasury, and had come to Jerusalem to worship, was returning. And sitting in his chariot, he was reading Isaiah the prophet.

Then the Spirit said to Philip, "Go near and overtake this chariot."

So Philip ran to him, and heard him reading the prophet Isaiah, and said, "Do you understand what you are reading?"

And he said, "How can I, unless someone guides me?" And he asked Philip to come up and sit with him.

MINISTERING BY THE ANOINTING

It's very important for every believer to learn to move and operate in the Spirit. Believers should boldly use the anointing God has placed on them to do the works Jesus did.

Jesus – Samaritan Woman

We have a wonderful example of Jesus operating in the revelation gifts of the Holy Spirit when He ministered to the woman at the well. Jesus operated in the supernatural revelation which came to Him through the Holy Spirit.

John 4:16-18,29,30,39 Jesus said to her, "Go, call your husband, and come here."

The woman answered and said, "I have no husband."

Jesus said to her, "You have well said, 'I have no husband,' for you have had five husbands, and the one whom you now have is not your husband; in that you spoke truly."

"Come, see a Man who told me all things that I ever did. Could this be the Christ?"

Then they went out of the city and came to Him.

And many of the Samaritans of that city believed in Him because of the word of the woman who testified, "He told me all that I ever did."

Paul – Spirit of Divination

Paul operated in the spiritual gift of the discerning of spirits by the anointing which was on him.

Acts 16:16-18 Now it happened, as we went to prayer, that a certain slave girl possessed with a spirit of divination met us, who brought her masters much profit by fortune-telling. This girl followed Paul and us, and cried out, saying, "These men are the servants of the Most High God, who proclaim to us the way of salvation."

And this she did for many days. But Paul, greatly annoyed, turned and said to the spirit, "I command you in the name of Jesus Christ to come out of her." And he came out that very hour.

Peter/John – Healing Lame Man

Peter and John ministered by the anointing of God when they ministered healing to the lame man at the temple gate.

Acts 3:1-9 Now Peter and John went up together to the temple at the hour of prayer, the ninth hour. And a certain man lame from his mother's womb was carried, whom they laid daily at the gate of the temple which is called Beautiful, to ask alms from those who entered

Miracle Evangelism

the temple; who, seeing Peter and John about to go into the temple, asked for alms.

And fixing his eyes on him, with John, Peter said, "Look at us." So he gave them his attention, expecting to receive something from them.

Then Peter said, "Silver and gold I do not have, but what I do have I give you: in the name of Jesus Christ of Nazareth, rise up and walk." And he took him by the right hand and lifted him up, and immediately his feet and ankle bones received strength. So he, leaping up, stood and walked and entered the temple with them–walking, leaping, and praising God. And all the people saw him walking and praising God.

In miracle evangelism, we need to be sensitive to the leading of the Holy Spirit. We need to let God reveal the root problem through revelation-knowledge. We need to boldly speak and release the power of God, the anointing, which is on us.

There are special graces and anointings given to those in the fivefold ministry to demonstrate supernatural revelation and power. However, the anointing and power to do the works of Jesus are for all believers.

All believers are anointed for miracle evangelism. They have the available anointing within them if they are obedient.

Philip at Samaria

Philip is a good example of a believer operating under the anointing of the Holy Spirit. Later in the book of Acts, we see Philip functioning in the fivefold ministry gifting of an evangelist. However, when he obeyed the words of Jesus to be His witness in Samaria, he was functioning as an ordinary believer, a deacon in the local church in Jerusalem.

Acts 8:4-8,12,13 Therefore those who were scattered went everywhere preaching the word.

Then Philip went down to the city of Samaria and preached Christ to them. And the multitudes with one accord heeded the things spoken by Philip, hearing and seeing the miracles which he did. For unclean spirits, crying with a loud voice, came out of many who were possessed; and many who were paralyzed and lame were healed. And there was great joy in that city.

But when they believed Philip as he preached the things concerning the kingdom of God and the name of Jesus Christ, both men and women were baptized.

Then Simon himself also believed; and when he was baptized he continued with Philip, and was amazed, seeing the miracles and signs which were done.

All believers have the anointing within them to win the lost. Believers who have received the baptism in the Holy

Spirit, and who are obedient to Jesus to be a bold witness, will experience a greater anointing of the Holy Spirit come on them – an anointing for powerful miracle evangelism. They, like Philip, will minister boldly in all nine gifts of the Holy Spirit. They, like Philip, will experience the same anointing which was on Jesus when He said, "The Spirit of the Lord is upon me, because He has anointed me to preach ..."

Reaching Our Cities

The church which seeks to reach its city needs to equip every believer to minister by the anointing of the Holy Spirit.

Isaiah 10:27 It shall come to pass in that day that his burden will be taken away from your shoulder, and his yoke from your neck, and the yoke will be destroyed because of the anointing oil.

As believers learn how to receive, flow with and minister in the anointing of God, they will become powerful, miracle-working soul winners for Jesus Christ!

QUESTIONS FOR REVIEW

1. What is the anointing?

2. Who is the anointing for?

3. What qualities will be present as we learn to flow with the Holy Spirit in our anointing?

Lesson Ten

The Gifts of the Spirit

GIVEN FOR MINISTRY

Every believer who would be effective in miracle evangelism must learn to operate in the gifts of the Holy Spirit.

When we reach out to the lost with the gospel, we must be aware that Jesus has a special gift for each one. This gift is a supernatural sign and will give us an open door to present the gospel.

Every person has special needs in his life. It may be sickness, inner hurts, rejections, or being tormented by demon spirits. God wants to meet a need in their life to confirm His word and to open their hearts to receive Him as their personal Savior. God is looking for "postmen" to deliver these gifts.

It's not that a believer has this gift or that gift, even though a believer may operate more freely in certain gifts than others. Instead, it's the person with the need, who receives one or another of these nine gifts of the Holy Spirit.

➢ People who are sick need the gifts of healings.

➢ Those suffering from deep inner hurts may need a word of knowledge.

➢ Those bound by demon spirits, need the gift of discerning of spirits to expose Satan's stronghold over their lives.

➢ People may need the working of miracles to reveal the power of the gospel to change their lives.

Paul said these gifts are given to each one.

1 Corinthians 12:7 But the manifestation of the Spirit is given to each one for the profit of all ...

Spirit-filled believers must operate in all nine gifts of the Holy Spirit to be effective in miracle evangelism. These gifts will open doors so that people will receive God's greatest gift – salvation through faith in His Son, Jesus.

Three Steps

There are three steps to effectively minister in the gifts of the Holy Spirit.

➢ **Know** – First, we need the revelation gifts so that we will know what God wants us to do.

➢ **Speak** – Second, we need the vocal gifts so that we can speak what God desires to say to a person, people, or situations.

> **Do** – Third we need the power gifts so that we can do what God desires us to do.

Nine Gifts

The apostle Paul listed the gifts of the Holy Spirit.

1 Corinthians 12:8-10 ... for to one is given the word of wisdom through the Spirit, to another the word of knowledge through the same Spirit, to another faith by the same Spirit, to another gifts of healings by the same Spirit, to another the working of miracles, to another prophecy, to another discerning of spirits, to another different kinds of tongues, to another the interpretation of tongues.

REVELATION GIFTS – TO KNOW

The revelation gifts are God revealing spirits, knowledge, or wisdom for a particular situation. These gifts can be given to us through the gifts of tongues and interpretation or the gift of prophecy. They may also come through visions, dreams, and an inner knowing.

Discerning of Spirits
> *Definition*

The discerning of spirits is a supernatural insight into the realm of the spirit world. It reveals the type of spirit or spirits behind a person, a situation, an action or a message. It's a knowing in the spirit which comes through supernatural revelation concerning the source, nature and activity of any spirit.

> *Three Areas*

There are three areas of spirit activity.

> The Spirit of God
> The human spirit
> Satan's kingdom

The Spirit of God is felt in the manifestation and impressions of Him and in the presence of heavenly angels sent to do battle for us and to bring His messages.

It's the human spirit which makes choices between the Holy Spirit and Satan's spirits, between good or evil. It can be a godly nature or a carnal nature.

The third spirit area which will be revealed is the evil presence of Satan or his demons.

> *In Ministry of Jesus*

When Peter answered Jesus and said, "You are the Christ, the Son of the living God," Jesus knew his statement wasn't made from human knowledge, but was revealed by the Father.

The Gifts of the Spirit

Matthew 16:16,17 And Simon Peter answered and said, "You are the Christ, the Son of the living God."

Jesus answered and said to him, "Blessed are you, Simon Bar-Jonah, for flesh and blood has not revealed this to you, but My Father who is in heaven."

A few moments later, Jesus discerned the spirit behind Peter's statement was Satan.

Matthew 16:22,23 Then Peter took Him aside and began to rebuke Him, saying, "Far be it from You, Lord; this shall not happen to You!"

But He turned and said to Peter, "Get behind Me, Satan! You are an offense to Me, for you are not mindful of the things of God, but the things of men."

➢ *In Miracle Evangelism*

The discerning of spirits is important in miracle evangelism because it's often necessary to do spiritual warfare. To set the captives free, we need to:

➢ discern right and wrong spirits

➢ know how they have attached themselves

➢ understand how they operated in the person's life

For example, when we are witnessing to a person, there may be spirits of lust, jealousy, pride, rebellion, witchcraft, familiar spirits or a combination of these and other demons. We need to know which spirits we are dealing with, and then we need to understand how they came into that person's life so that they can be set free.

Every evil spirit discerned must be bound and cast out. We are to take action!

Luke 10:19,20 "Behold, I give you the authority to trample on serpents and scorpions, and over all the power of the enemy, and nothing shall by any means hurt you. Nevertheless do not rejoice in this, that the spirits are subject to you, but rather rejoice because your names are written in heaven."

Word of Knowledge
➢ *Definition*

The word of knowledge is a supernatural revelation by the Holy Spirit of certain facts, present or past, about a person, or situation which are not learned through the natural mind.

It's a small part of the total knowledge of any given situation. God only shares partial knowledge.

➢ *In Ministry of Jesus*

When Jesus talked to the woman at the well, this one manifestation of the word of knowledge stirred and caused a revival in Samaria.

John 4:16,18,39,41,42 Jesus said to her, "Go, call your husband, and come here."

"For you have had five husbands, and the one whom you now have is not your husband; in that you spoke truly."

And many of the Samaritans of that city believed in Him because of the word of the woman who testified, "He told me all that I ever did."

And many more believed because of His own word.

Then they said to the woman, "Now we believe, not because of what you said, for we have heard for ourselves and know that this is indeed the Christ, the Savior of the world."

➢ *In Miracle Evangelism*

Through the gift of the word of knowledge, we will learn certain facts supernaturally. This information will help us minister to the needs of the person in greater boldness.

The word of knowledge works together with the discerning of spirits by revealing facts, present or past, about a person or situation.

The word of knowledge may reveal:

➢ names of diseases
➢ names of people or relationships
➢ a person whom we should call or visit
➢ incidences and circumstances of the past which could only be known by supernatural revelation

The word of knowledge operates when we are bringing the gospel to the lost.

We may:

➢ see something in the spirit around a person or a place
➢ hear a word or a phrase in the spirit
➢ feel in our own body a manifestation of something concerning another person

Word of Wisdom
➢ *Definition*

The word of wisdom is a supernatural revelation given to the believer. It's God's wisdom to proceed on a course of action based on natural or supernatural knowledge. It reveals God's plan and purpose:

➢ for our lives and ministries
➢ to be done immediately or in the future
➢ on how an individual or corporate body should proceed in God's will

Many Forms

The word of wisdom comes in many forms:

- an inner voice
- through a vision when awake
- through dreams when asleep
- through operating in the vocal gifts

In Ministry of Jesus

Jesus operated in the word of wisdom when He talked with the rich young ruler.

Matthew 19:16,17,21 Now behold, one came and said to Him, "Good Teacher, what good thing shall I do that I may have eternal life?"

So He said to him, "Why do you call Me good? No one is good but One, that is, God. But if you want to enter into life, keep the commandments." Jesus said to him, "If you want to be perfect, go, sell what you have and give to the poor, and you will have treasure in heaven; and come, follow Me."

In Miracle Evangelism

God may tell us something about a person who is a complete stranger through a word of knowledge. Then He gives supernatural wisdom on how to proceed.

If we flow in the gifts of the Spirit, God can use them to convince unbelievers that He is God – that He cares for them – that they can have salvation.

The word of wisdom operates closely with the gift of discerning of spirits and the word of knowledge so that we may be able to minister to people. It's revelation of how to minister to a particular need. The word of wisdom creates faith to minister boldly.

The word of wisdom is given for protection and instruction and often reveals to us how to apply knowledge revealed through the word of knowledge. It may give an insight to pray in a certain way.

The word of wisdom may instruct us to:

- lay hands on a person
- speak a word
- perform a creative miracle
- cast out a demon

The word of wisdom gives us the wisdom to effectively present the gospel in every situation.

WHAT TO SPEAK – VOCAL GIFTS

When we receive a word of knowledge about someone or a situation, it could be spoken through tongues, interpretation of tongues or prophecy. When we receive a revelation, we need to open our spirit, to check our inward witness, as to whether we should speak or pray about the revelation.

Many times through the vocal gifts we can receive information concerning the person we are ministering to. This is a supernatural revelation so that the person can receive. "God shows me that you have ...

➢ specific detail about a person's past ...
➢ specific details about a present situation or circumstances."

Specific revelation will create faith both in the person ministering and in the person being ministered to.

Gift of Tongues
➢ *Definition*

The gift of tongues is a supernatural expression or inspiration by the Holy Spirit using our physical voice organs. It's a language never learned by the speaker, nor understood by the mind of the speaker. The spoken message may be a heavenly language used by the angels, or a human language. The gift of tongues may be a language which is understood by a listener.

➢ *In Miracle Evangelism*

The gift of tongues has been one gift many people would like to hide. But the apostle Paul wrote that it was a sign to the unbeliever.

1 Corinthians 14:22 Therefore tongues are for a sign, not to those who believe but to unbelievers; but prophesying is not for unbelievers but for those who believe.

On the day of Pentecost the gift of tongues was instrumental in bringing thousands to Christ. The gift of tongues was part of the first evangelistic effort.

Acts 2:6 And when this sound occurred, the multitude came together, and were confused, because everyone heard them speak in his own language.

Interpretation of Tongues
➢ *Definition*

The gift of interpretation of tongues is the supernatural showing forth by the Spirit of the explanation, or meaning, in the hearer's own language, of a vocal expression of a message in another tongue. It's not an operation or understanding of the mind. It's given by the Spirit of God.

Interpretation means to explain, expound, or unfold. It's usually not a literal, word for word, translation.

➢ *In Miracle Evangelism*

The gift of interpretation flows with the gift of tongues. If God led you to pray in tongues with an unbeliever, they probably would not know what you were doing. However, when the gift of interpretation began to operate and you began speaking forth things you could not know naturally, it would be a definite sign to them of God's presence.

Gift of Prophecy
➢ *Definition*

The gift of prophecy is a spontaneous, supernatural vocal expression of inspiration in a known tongue which strengthens, encourages, and comforts the body of Christ. It's a direct message from God to a particular person or group of people.

The Greek word for prophecy is "propheteia" meaning speaking the mind and counsel of God.

➢ *In Miracle Evangelism*

The gift of prophecy could work the same way in an unbeliever's life as the gift of tongues and interpretation. It would be a speaking forth of things you could not know in the natural and therefore a sign of the presence of God.

POWER GIFTS – TO DO

The power gifts are the manifestation of God's power through us. These power gifts are the gift of faith, the gifts of healings, and the working of miracles.

The word of wisdom always releases the gift of faith to work. When we know what God wants done by a word of wisdom, we will become bold to operate in the gift of faith, the working of miracles and the gifts of healings.

Gift of Faith
➢ *Definition*

The gift of faith is a supernatural faith for a specific time and purpose. It's a gift of power to accomplish a certain task in whatever situation we are in at a particular time. When the word of wisdom is given telling us how to do a certain task, it will spark the gift of faith to boldly carry out the task according to what God has already planned.

➢ *How to Receive*

The gift of faith is received by the operation of the revelation gifts. When the gift of faith comes, the believer does not strive to believe. He knows what is getting ready to happen and boldly acts on revelation-knowledge. The result of the gift of faith is the working of miracles and the gifts of healings.

> *In Ministry of Jesus*

Jesus said He only did what He saw the Father doing. When He saw the dead man being carried out, He must have seen the Father speaking to that man and the man coming back to life.

Luke 7:12-15 And when He came near the gate of the city, behold, a dead man was being carried out, the only son of his mother; and she was a widow. And a large crowd from the city was with her.

When the Lord saw her, He had compassion on her and said to her, "Do not weep." Then He came and touched the open coffin, and those who carried him stood still. And He said, "Young man, I say to you, arise."

And he who was dead sat up and began to speak. And He presented him to his mother.

When Jesus calmed the great storm, we have another example of the gift of faith in action.

Mark 4:37-41 And a great windstorm arose, and the waves beat into the boat, so that it was already filling. But He was in the stern, asleep on a pillow. And they awoke Him and said to Him, "Teacher, do You not care that we are perishing?"

Then He arose and rebuked the wind, and said to the sea, "Peace, be still!" And the wind ceased and there was a great calm. But He said to them, "Why are you so fearful? How is it that you have no faith?"

And they feared exceedingly, and said to one another, "Who can this be, that even the wind and the sea obey Him!"

> *In Miracle Evangelism*

However difficult the condition may look, God will supernaturally drop into our spirits the faith to lay our hands on the sick and speak a creative miracle. When the gift of the word of wisdom operates, we will see God perform a miracle and the gift of faith will rise in our spirits. Then we can move into the gift of working of miracles.

Working of Miracles
> *Definition*

The working of miracles is a supernatural intervention of God in the ordinary course of nature. It's the supernatural demonstration of the power of God by which the laws of nature are altered, suspended or controlled.

It's just as easy to work a miracle as it is to give a message in tongues. Often we receive a word of knowledge and then a word of wisdom which reveals what God wants us to do with that knowledge. When we receive the word of

The Gifts of the Spirit

wisdom we see ourselves working a miracle. Suddenly, the gift of faith is released and we boldly work out what we have just seen in the Spirit. It's for this reason that it's called the working of miracles. Miracles always confirm the word of God and glorify Jesus.

➢ *In Life of Jesus*

When Jesus fed thousands with seven loaves of bread and a few little fish, we have a wonderful example of the working of miracles.

Matthew 15:33-38 Then His disciples said to Him, "Where could we get enough bread in the wilderness to fill such a great multitude?"

Jesus said to them, "How many loaves do you have?"

And they said, "Seven, and a few little fish."

And He commanded the multitude to sit down on the ground. And He took the seven loaves and the fish and gave thanks, broke them and gave them to His disciples; and the disciples gave to the multitude.

So they all ate and were filled, and they took up seven large baskets full of the fragments that were left. Now those who ate were four thousand men, besides women and children.

➢ *In Miracle Evangelism*

There are many reasons for the working of miracles.

➢ Protection
➢ Deliverance from danger
➢ Providing to those in want
➢ Carrying out judgment
➢ Confirming the calling of a person
➢ Confirming word which has been preached

When we operate in the supernatural on a regular basis, the lost of this world will take notice and want a relationship with our powerful, loving, miracle-working God.

Gifts of Healings
➢ *Definition*

The gifts of healings are the supernatural impartations of God's healing power into people who need healing. They are described as gifts (plural) because there are many ways to impart, or minister healing to the sick. The person receiving the healing has received the gifts of healings. The gifts of healings are supernatural manifestations of the Holy Spirit and are not the same as medical science.

They are God's gifts to the body of Christ and in particular to the one needing the healing.

87

Miracle Evangelism

➢ *In Life of Jesus*

The four gospels are full of accounts of Jesus ministering to people in the gifts of healings. Likewise, the book of Acts, is full of accounts of how the early believers operated in the gifts of healings as well as the other gifts of the Holy Spirit. Each time miracles took place, people came to Jesus. Jesus said believers would lay hands on the sick and they would recover. This, Jesus said, would be one of the signs that would confirm His word to a lost world.

➢ *In Miracle Evangelism*

Often demon spirits of infirmity are responsible for the person's sickness. For example, there are spirits of cancer, arthritis, resentment and bitterness.

By the discerning of spirits, the Holy Spirit will reveal the source of the problem and the person can be delivered. The discerning of spirits will come by an impression or a thought which reveals the name of the spirit of infirmity which is the source of the problem.

Matthew 9:32,33 As they went out, behold, they brought to Him a man, mute and demon-possessed. And when the demon was cast out, the mute spoke. And the multitudes marveled, saying, "It was never seen like this in Israel!"

When we know from the Lord what the problem in a person's life is, it's easy to minister gifts of healings to that person. When a person has been healed in the name of Jesus, it opens the door for the person to know Him and accept Him as his or her personal Savior.

Summary

The gifts of healings, as in the ministry of Jesus and the apostles, are the most important supernatural manifestations for effective miracle evangelism. When God confirms His word through miracles of healing, people always come to Jesus.

No longer are the gifts of the Holy Spirit limited to the ministry of a few healing evangelists. The days of the superstars are over. This is the day of every believer doing the works of Jesus – every believer will be a miracle-working witness for Jesus Christ in their daily life.

When every Spirit-filled believer flows and operates by God's anointing in each of the gifts of the Holy Spirit, a wave of miracle evangelism will sweep across our cities and around the world.

*For in-depth study on the gifts of the Holy Spirit, read **Supernatural Living Through the Gifts of the Holy Spirit** by A.L. and Joyce Gill and **Victory Over Deception** by Joyce Gill.*

QUESTIONS FOR REVIEW

1. What are three steps to effectively minister in the gifts of the Spirit?

2. What are the three categories of the gifts of the Spirit?

3. List the nine gifts of the Spirit and how they are to be used in miracle evangelism.

Lesson Eleven

Ministering Healing and Deliverance

There are many ways to minister to the sick and demon possessed. In the Gospels and the book of Acts, we see the different ways Jesus ministered to the needs of people.

Everyone involved in miracle evangelism must be led by the Spirit. Even when a Christian is healed, unbelievers hear about it. Every healing, deliverance and miracle should lead unbelievers to believe and receive Jesus as their Savior.

GOD'S HEALING POWER

Woman Healed

As we study the healing ministry of Jesus, we discover that there was a healing power in His body which could flow out and heal others. An example of this is found in the story of the woman with the issue of blood.

Mark 5:25-34 Now a certain woman had a flow of blood for twelve years, and had suffered many things from many physicians. She had spent all that she had and was no better, but rather grew worse.

When she heard about Jesus, she came behind Him in the crowd and touched His garment; for she said, "If only I may touch His clothes, I shall be made well." Immediately the fountain of her blood was dried up, and she felt in her body that she was healed of the affliction.

And Jesus, immediately knowing in Himself that power had gone out of Him, turned around in the crowd and said, "Who touched My clothes?"

But His disciples said to Him, "You see the multitude thronging You, and You say, 'Who touched Me?'"

And He looked around to see her who had done this thing.

But the woman, fearing and trembling, knowing what had happened to her, came and fell down before Him and told Him the whole truth.

And He said to her, "Daughter, your faith has made you well. Go in peace, and be healed of your affliction."

The Greek word used for the "power" which flowed from Jesus into this woman is "dunamis." It's the root word from which we have our English word "dynamite."

Dynamite Power

Jesus stopped and turned around when the woman touched Him because He felt dynamite power flow from His body. The power of the Holy Spirit which came on Jesus when He was baptized in the Jordan River, was a real and tangible power which was transferred by touching.

Luke 6:19 And the whole multitude sought to touch Him, for power went out from Him and healed them all.

Jesus said that we would receive power when the Holy Spirit came on us.

Act 1:8 "But you shall receive power when the Holy Spirit has come upon you; and you shall be witnesses to Me in Jerusalem, and in all Judea and Samaria, and to the end of the earth."

The word used for "power" is exactly the same word which was used to describe the power which flowed from Jesus. Spirit-filled believers have exactly the same power which was in Jesus!

We have the same dynamite power on the inside of us. As we minister healing, we simply release this power to flow into the lives of others.

John 7:38 "He who believes in Me, as the Scripture has said, out of his heart will flow rivers of living water."

The dynamite power within us will flow out to others when we obey God.

Through Faith

The woman with the issue of blood, had spent all her money on doctors who had been unable to help her. In the midst of her desperate situation, she heard about Jesus. Faith came into her spirit when she heard of the miracles He had done.

Romans 10:17 So then faith comes by hearing, and hearing by the word of God.

She began to speak her faith as she boldly declared, "If only I may touch His clothes, I shall be made well." Then she began to act on that faith as she reached out and touched His clothes. At that moment, the healing power that was in Jesus flowed into her body and she was healed.

Jesus said to her, "Daughter, your faith has made you well!"

As we obey God and lay our hands on the sick, we too by faith, must release the mighty healing power of God which is within us, to flow into the bodies of those who need to be healed. We will find ourselves boldly speaking our faith and acting our faith as did the woman with the issue of blood.

Laying on of Hands
➢ *By Jesus*

Jesus laid hands on the leper, and the power which was in Him flowed into the man.

Ministering Healing and Deliverance

Mark 1:40,41 Then a leper came to Him, imploring Him, kneeling down to Him and saying to Him, "If You are willing, You can make me clean." And Jesus, moved with compassion, put out His hand and touched him, and said to him, "I am willing; be cleansed."

To heal the deaf and mute man, Jesus put His fingers in his ears.

Mark 7:31-35 And again, departing from the region of Tyre and Sidon, He came through the midst of the region of Decapolis to the Sea of Galilee. Then they brought to Him one who was deaf and had an impediment in his speech, and they begged Him to put His hand on him. And He took him aside from the multitude, and put His fingers in his ears, and He spat and touched his tongue. Then, looking up to heaven, He sighed, and said to him, "Ephphatha," that is, "Be opened."

Immediately his ears were opened, and the impediment of his tongue was loosed, and he spoke plainly.

Jesus usually placed His hands on the area needing healing.

➤ *By Paul*

The apostle Paul laid hands on the sick and they recovered.

Acts 19:11 Now God worked unusual miracles by the hands of Paul ...

Acts 28:8 And it happened that the father of Publius lay sick of a fever and dysentery. Paul went in to him and prayed, and he laid his hands on him and healed him.

➤ *All believers*

All believers were commanded to lay their hands on the sick and they would recover.

Mark 16:17,18 "And these signs will follow those who believe: in My name they will cast out demons; they will speak with new tongues; they will take up serpents; and if they drink anything deadly, it will by no means hurt them; they will lay hands on the sick, and they will recover."

Speaking Name of Jesus

There is tremendous power released when we speak the name of Jesus.

➤ *By Peter and John*

Acts 3:1-8,16 Now Peter and John went up together to the temple at the hour of prayer, the ninth hour. And a certain man lame from his mother's womb was carried, whom they laid daily at the gate of the temple which is called Beautiful, to ask alms from those who entered the temple; who, seeing Peter and John about to go into the temple, asked for alms.

Miracle Evangelism

And fixing his eyes on him, with John, Peter said, "Look at us." So he gave them his attention, expecting to receive something from them.

Then Peter said, "Silver and gold I do not have, but what I do have I give you: in the name of Jesus Christ of Nazareth, rise up and walk."

And he took him by the right hand and lifted him up, and immediately his feet and ankle bones received strength. So he, leaping up, stood and walked and entered the temple with them— walking, leaping, and praising God.

Peter said it was the name of Jesus which had made the man whole.

v. 16 "And His name, through faith in His name, has made this man strong, whom you see and know. Yes, the faith which comes through Him has given him this perfect soundness in the presence of you all."

➢ *Boldness to Continue*

The apostles prayed for boldness to continue to speak in the name of Jesus when their lives were threatened if they did so.

Acts 4:29-31 "Now, Lord, look on their threats, and grant to Your servants that with all boldness they may speak Your word, by stretching out Your hand to heal, and that signs and wonders may be done through the name of Your holy Servant Jesus."

And when they had prayed, the place where they were assembled together was shaken; and they were all filled with the Holy Spirit, and they spoke the word of God with boldness.

Speak the name of Jesus with authority. Speak healing in His name.

Speak to Spirits of Infirmity

While ministering to the sick, power is transmitted by the contact of the laying on of hands. Faith is often released by the words which we speak.

Many illnesses are caused by demon spirits of infirmity which have attached themselves to the body.

Luke 13:11,16 And behold, there was a woman who had a spirit of infirmity eighteen years, and was bent over and could in no way raise herself up.

"So ought not this woman, being a daughter of Abraham, whom Satan has bound–think of it–for eighteen years, be loosed from this bond on the Sabbath?"

Jesus referred to sickness as a bondage. Jesus cast out the demon spirit of infirmity and the woman was healed.

➢ *Incurable Diseases*

Diseases which medical science call incurable are usually caused by spirits of infirmity. In ministering to these

Ministering Healing and Deliverance

cases, either speak to the spirit of infirmity or call them by the specific name of the disease.

Examples of "incurable diseases" caused by spirits today are cancer, leukemia, and arthritis. There are also biblical examples of spirits causing sickness and infirmity.

➢ *Dumb Spirit*

Matthew 9:32 As they went out, behold, they brought to Him a man, mute and demon-possessed.

➢ *Deaf Spirit*

Mark 9:25 When Jesus saw that the people came running together, He rebuked the unclean spirit, saying to him, "You deaf and dumb spirit, I command you, come out of him, and enter him no more!"

➢ *Spirit of Insanity*

Matthew 17:15,18 "Lord, have mercy on my son, for he is an epileptic and suffers severely; for he often falls into the fire and often into the water. And Jesus rebuked the demon, and he came out of him; and the child was cured from that very hour."

➢ *Spirit of Blindness*

Matthew 12:22 Then one was brought to Him who was demon-possessed, blind and mute; and He healed him, so that the blind and mute man both spoke and saw.

Binding and Loosing

We are to minister healing by binding and loosing.

Matthew 16:19 "And I will give you the keys of the kingdom of heaven, and whatever you bind on earth will be bound in heaven, and whatever you loose on earth will be loosed in heaven."

To bind means to constrain, to tie up, or limit the ability to act. We can say:

>"I bind you Satan over this person's body ..."
>
>"I bind you spirit of cancer ..."

To loose means to release the person from the bondage of the disease.

Luke 13:12 But when Jesus saw her, He called her to Him and said to her, "Woman, you are loosed from your infirmity."

Mark 16:17a "And these signs will follow those who believe: in My name they will cast out demons."

For example, we can command, "In the name of Jesus, you spirit of cancer come out of him."

Creative Miracles

Creative miracles were an important part of the ministry of Jesus, and He said, "The works that I do shall you do also."

Jesus spoke a creative miracle to the man with the withered hand.

Mark 3:1,3,5b And He entered the synagogue again, and a man was there who had a withered hand.

Then He said to the man who had the withered hand, "Step forward."

He said to the man, "Stretch out your hand." And he stretched it out, and his hand was restored as whole as the other.

Some people have parts of their bodies missing through surgery, accidents, deteriorating diseases or birth defects. We, like Jesus can release our faith to minister creative miracles by speaking and commanding the part of the body which is missing to be restored.

Mark 11:23 "For assuredly, I say to you, whoever says to this mountain, 'Be removed and be cast into the sea,' and does not doubt in his heart, but believes that those things he says will come to pass, he will have whatever he says."

God's Not Reluctant

For years, we have been praying as though we have been begging a reluctant God to heal the sick. This verse does not say that we are to pray. It says we are to say. Jesus has given us authority over all of the power of the enemy. We were created to take dominion on this earth. Now, we must boldly do the works of Jesus. Jesus said we were to heal the sick. He did not say we were to ask Him to do it.

Matthew 10:8 "Heal the sick, cleanse the lepers, raise the dead, cast out demons. Freely you have received, freely give."

No matter how impossible the situation may seem, we know that "all things are possible with God" and that "everything is possible for him who believes."

Our immediate response when someone comes to us and needs a creative miracle should be, "Oh, that's easy with God!"

When we need miracle-working faith, beyond where ours has grown by hearing the word, we must be sensitive to the Holy Spirit. If this is the time for a creative miracle to take place, God will give us a word of wisdom and we will see the miracle taking place before we minister. The gift of faith will be released and we will boldly speak to the mountain.

Matthew 17:20 So Jesus said to them, "Because of your unbelief; for assuredly, I say to you, if you have faith as a mustard seed, you will say to this mountain, 'Move from here to there,' and it will move; and nothing will be impossible for you."

As we speak with authority, we must boldly command the body to be restored to normal. We might say:

"I speak a new heart into this body!"

"I command these fingers to grow out!"

Jesus spoke boldly and forcibly in His miracle-working ministry.

Acts 14:8-10 And in Lystra a certain man without strength in his feet was sitting, a cripple from his mother's womb, who had never walked.

This man heard Paul speaking. Paul, observing him intently and seeing that he had faith to be healed, said with a loud voice, "Stand up straight on your feet!" And he leaped and walked.

Speaking the Word

Another powerful way of ministering healing to the sick is by speaking the word of God. Jesus said that the greatest example of faith He had ever found was in the centurion whose servant was paralyzed and in terrible suffering.

The centurion had just said to Jesus, "Just speak the word only, and my servant will be healed!"

It's important that we don't speak our doubts or our feelings, but that we speak only the word. When we speak the word, we are sending the word into action in a person's life.

Psalms 107:20 He sent His word and healed them, and delivered them from their destructions.

The words that we speak, have the power to destroy or to bring life and health.

Proverbs 18:21 Death and life are in the power of the tongue.

When we send the word of God into action in a person's life, we see mighty miracles.

Isaiah 55:11 So shall My word be that goes forth from My mouth; it shall not return to Me void, but it shall accomplish what I please, and it shall prosper in the thing for which I sent it.

Acting on Word of God

Jesus said, "I only do what I see my Father doing."

We too must be sensitive to the Holy Spirit and then boldly act on what He has shown us. There is no room for timidity or fear in effective miracle evangelism.

2 Timothy 1:7 For God has not given us a spirit of fear, but of power and of love and of a sound mind.

We must not be afraid of looking foolish or of losing our reputation. If Jesus didn't need a reputation, then we don't need to be concerned about ours.

Philippians 2:7 ... but made Himself of no reputation, taking the form of a servant, and coming in the likeness of men.

The devil will try to put the thought in our minds, "What if you minister to someone, and they don't get healed? Won't you look foolish?"

Instead, we must boldly say, "Jesus said it. I believe it. Therefore I choose to obey the words of Jesus."

Mark 16:18b *"They will lay hands on the sick, and they will recover."*

Immediately after we release the healing power of God into a person's body, we should get them to move their faith into action. We should tell them to do what they couldn't do before – to boldly act on the word.

"Bend over and touch your toes!"

"Move around and check out your body!"

Confidently ask, "What happened to the pain?"

Jesus told the man with the withered hand, "Stretch out your hand!" He told the lame man, "Take up your bed and walk!"

As Spirit-filled believers, we have the same healing power in us which was in Jesus. As we lay our hands on the sick, we by faith release healing power of the Holy Spirit into the bodies of those who need healing. As we boldly speak the name of Jesus, cast out spirits of infirmity, and speak creative miracles into people, God will confirm His word with great healing miracles. Each time people are healed, God's word is confirmed and people will come to know Jesus.

God is restoring miracle evangelism to the church, and we are finding ourselves once again living in exciting days, just as they were recorded in the book of Acts.

*For in-depth study on the subject of healing, read **God's Provision for Healing** by A.L. and Joyce Gill*

QUESTIONS FOR REVIEW

1. How can we release the healing power that is within us, to flow into others who need healing?

2. List four ways of speaking that releases the healing power of God.

3. How do we minister healing when a creative miracle is needed?

4. How are we to instruct people who need healing, so that we can move their faith into action?

Lesson Twelve

Finances and the Pioneer Spirit

FINANCES FOR REVIVAL

The Holy Spirit emphasized prosperity in the 1980's to equip the church economically for the global harvest which is coming in the 1990's.

The reality is that it takes billions of dollars to fulfill the Great Commission. Evangelistic endeavors take money – missions advances take money.

The Holy Spirit emphasized prosperity in the Bible to liberate us from debt and to equip us financially for this final global harvest.

Early Church

We often hear about the early church selling everything they had and giving it to God.

Acts 4:32-35 Now the multitude of those who believed were of one heart and one soul; neither did anyone say that any of the things he possessed was his own, but they had all things in common. And with great power the apostles gave witness to the resurrection of the Lord Jesus. And great grace was upon them all. Nor was there anyone among them who lacked; for all who were possessors of lands or houses sold them, and brought the proceeds of the things that were sold, and laid them at the apostles' feet; and they distributed to each as anyone had need.

It's interesting to note that right in the middle of this story about the spirit of giving which permeated the early church, we find these important words, "With great power the apostles gave witness to the resurrection of the Lord Jesus."

Barnabas, an Example
➢ *Gave All – Sowing*

Barnabas was one who sold all that he owned and brought the money to the apostles. He invested it in world evangelism.

Acts 4:36,37 And Joses, who was also named Barnabas by the apostles (which is translated Son of Encouragement), a Levite of the country of Cyprus, having land, sold it, and brought the money and laid it at the apostles' feet.

➢ *Reaping Faith*

We hear of Barnabas again when he was selected to go to Antioch. The Scripture says, "He was a good man, full of the Holy Spirit and of faith."

Miracle Evangelism

Acts 11:22b-24 ... they sent out Barnabas to go as far as Antioch. When he came and had seen the grace of God, he was glad, and encouraged them all that with purpose of heart they should continue with the Lord. For he was a good man, full of the Holy Spirit and of faith.

➢ *Reaping Souls*

v. 24b And a great many people were added to the Lord.

➢ *Reaping Ministry*

It was Barnabas who went to get Saul and brought him into his ministry. Barnabas and Saul taught for a whole year making disciples at Antioch.

Acts 11:25,26 Then Barnabas departed for Tarsus to seek Saul. And when he had found him, he brought him to Antioch. So it was that for a whole year they assembled with the church and taught a great many people. And the disciples were first called Christians in Antioch.

➢ *Reaping Anointing*

Paul and Barnabas were set apart by the Holy Spirit for the work He had called them to. They were sent out to teach and preach.

Acts 13:2-5a As they ministered to the Lord and fasted, the Holy Spirit said, "Now separate to Me Barnabas and Saul for the work to which I have called them."

Then, having fasted and prayed, and laid hands on them, they sent them away. So, being sent out by the Holy Spirit, they went down to Seleucia, and from there they sailed to Cyprus. And when they arrived in Salamis, they preached the word of God in the synagogues of the Jews.

➢ *Reaping Finances*

From the time Barnabas gave all that he had we don't hear of him working for money again. He did not have any financial resources – he had given all he had to the Lord. He had been faithful to sow seed into the gospel. Now Barnabas was reaping what he had sown as finances for his own miracle ministry. Barnabas had all the finances he needed to obey the Holy Spirit and go into all the world and preach the gospel.

LAW OF SOWING AND REAPING

God desires that we understand the rhythm of sowing and reaping and sowing again in greater measure. It's a principle which He has weaved into the fabric of the universe.

World missions is certainly a good work. God desires that we have abundance to sow into missions. Spiritually or financially we cannot impart what we don't possess.

Instructions to Timothy

Paul wrote to Timothy:

1 Timothy 6:17-19 Command those who are rich in this present age not to be haughty, nor to trust in uncertain riches but in the living God, who gives us richly all things to enjoy.

➢ *Sowing*

v. 18 Let them do good, that they be rich in good works, ready to give, willing to share.

➢ *Reaping*

v. 19 storing up for themselves a good foundation for the time to come, that they may lay hold on eternal life.

➢ *Stewards*

Christians are the stewards of the blessings of God because ultimately everything belongs to Him.

1 Peter 4:10 As each one has received a gift, minister it to one another, as good stewards of the manifold grace of God.

The early church pioneers volunteered to go to the world, sold their possessions, and started for the field. They were possessed with a passion to go to the end of the world for their Lord. No sacrifice seemed to be too great for them for the gospel to be proclaimed.

We must target our faith to give for the work of the Lord and then we will fulfill the Great Commission. World evangelism is the primary purpose for the financial prosperity which God has promised.

Farmer Sows and Reaps

When a farmer plants his seed he does not get back just one seed. A seed of corn produces a stalk of corn, the stalk produces several ears of corn and each new ear produces hundreds of seeds.

The farmer had to sow before he could get a harvest. The more seeds he has sown the larger the harvest is.

2 Corinthians 9:6,7,10 But this I say: He who sows sparingly will also reap sparingly, and he who sows bountifully will also reap bountifully.

Miracle Evangelism

So let each one give as he purposes in his heart, not grudgingly or of necessity; for God loves a cheerful giver.

God has promised to supply both the seed to sow and the provision we need for our daily lives.

v. 10 Now may He who supplies seed to the sower, and bread for food, supply and multiply the seed you have sown and increase the fruits of your righteousness.

➤ *Our Choice*

We have the choice either to sow our seed or eat it. When we sow our seed and exercise our faith, we release God's law of sowing and reaping.

Deuteronomy 26:13,14 "... then you shall say before the Lord your God: 'I have removed the holy tithe from my house, and also have given them to the Levite, the stranger, the fatherless, and the widow, according to all Your commandments which You have commanded me; I have not transgressed Your commandments, nor have I forgotten them. I have not eaten any of it when in mourning, nor have I removed any of it for any unclean use, nor given any of it for the dead. I have obeyed the voice of the Lord my God, and have done according to all that You have commanded me.' "

King Solomon warned us that if we are ruled by our circumstances, we will never sow.

Ecclesiastes 11:4 He who observes the wind will not sow, and he who regards the clouds will not reap.

➤ *Sowing Morning and Evening*

We must sow regularly into every good work – the preaching of the gospel of the Lord Jesus Christ.

Ecclesiastes 11:6 In the morning sow your seed, and in the evening do not withhold your hand; for you do not know which will prosper, either this or that, or whether both alike will be good.

Sowing in Flesh or Spirit

Paul states that we will reap whatever we sow.

Galatians 6:6-9 Let him who is taught the word share in all good things with him who teaches.

Do not be deceived, God is not mocked; for whatever a man sows, that he will also reap. For he who sows to his flesh will of the flesh reap corruption, but he who sows to the Spirit will of the Spirit reap everlasting life.

And let us not grow weary while doing good, for in due season we shall reap if we do not lose heart.

God's law of prosperity:

➤ sow the seed
➤ in due season we will reap

Finances and the Pioneer Spirit

➢ the kind of seed we sow is what we harvest

As we sow our seed in the gospel of Jesus Christ, we will reap His harvest. God will take our seed and multiply it back to us.

Notice the timing of our harvest – in due season. We will reap what we sow. If we sow money, we will reap money. We cannot sow good deeds and expect God to return finances. If we desire more wealth to reach the lost and more money to meet our needs, then we must put more money into the kingdom of God.

PIONEER SPIRIT

The pioneer spirit is a force which opens new trails that others can follow. The early church was an explosion which hit a world bound by legalistic traditions. The pioneer spirit is one which pushes outward at any cost and one that breaks new ground.

The pioneer has always been called to a rough, challenging, dangerous adventure.

Greatness is built on the work of those who break new ground.

The pioneers of the New Testament church brought the church through new barriers, established gifts and released men and women to the work of Christ Jesus. The force of the New Testament church was its growth and its thrust in world evangelism.

The Restoration

God is re-establishing pioneer, miracle evangelism in the church. There is a compelling in the spirits of men and women to move and invade new frontiers.

God, through Jesus, set the example for pioneer evangelism. Jesus went with His disciples from one place to another refusing to stay long in one place because others had not heard the gospel.

Our Examples
➢ *Paul*

The apostle Paul is certainly an example of the pioneer spirit. He was:

➢ A spiritual trouble-maker to traditionalists
➢ A headache to religious leaders
➢ A breaker of legalistic rules
➢ The father of New Testament pioneers

Before Paul's conversion, he was one-hundred percent committed to destroying the church. When he accepted

Jesus as his Savior, he was one-hundred percent committed to advancing the kingdom of God.

When others were boasting of the things they had done, Paul wrote a summary of the things he had been through for the sake of the gospel and yet, he said he had nothing to boast about.

2 Corinthians 11:23 Are they ministers of Christ?–I speak as a fool–I am more:

> in labors more abundant,
> in stripes above measure,
> in prisons more frequently,
> in deaths often.
> From the Jews five times I received forty stripes minus one.
> Three times I was beaten with rods;
> once I was stoned;
> three times I was shipwrecked;
> a night and a day I have been in the deep;
> in journeys often,
> in perils of waters,
> in perils of robbers,
> in perils of my own countrymen,
> in perils of the Gentiles,
> in perils in the city,
> in perils in the wilderness,
> in perils in the sea,
> in perils among false brethren;
> in weariness and toil,
> in sleeplessness often,
> in hunger and thirst,
> in fastings often,
> in cold and nakedness–
> besides the other things, what comes upon me daily:
> my deep concern for all the churches.

➤ *The Apostles*

Even when threatened with death and beatings, the apostles went daily to the temple (public) and to every house (private) teaching and preaching Jesus.

Acts 5:40-42 And they agreed with him, and when they had called for the apostles and beaten them, they commanded that they should not speak in the name of Jesus, and let them go. So they departed from the presence of the council, rejoicing that they were counted worthy to suffer shame for His name. And daily in the temple, and in every house, they did not cease teaching and preaching Jesus as the Christ.

➤ *Persecuted Believers*

Stephen became the first martyr. He taught the word of God even while he was facing death. What a testimony he presented to the man who later became the apostle Paul.

When the persecution increased, the believers scattered to protect their families from prison and death. But what did they do? Were they quiet about their faith so that they could live comfortable lives? No, they went everywhere preaching the word.

Acts 8:1-4 Now Saul was consenting to his death. At that time a great persecution arose against the church which was at Jerusalem; and they were all scattered throughout the regions of Judea and Samaria, except the apostles. And devout men carried Stephen to his burial, and made great lamentation over him.

As for Saul, he made havoc of the church, entering every house, and dragging off men and women, committing them to prison.

Therefore those who were scattered went everywhere preaching the word.

The church has always been the strongest and has flourished in evangelistic outreaches during its times of greatest persecution.

GOD'S PLAN

God's plan for building the body of Christ has not changed. The early church obeyed the Great Commission and went about everywhere doing the works of Jesus – healing the sick, teaching and preaching the good news of the kingdom. They continued in the face of persecution, even to their deaths.

The church has always been healthy when its vision was outward and least healthy when its energies are devoted to itself.

Ministry Teams

Jesus sent the seventy disciples out in teams of two. Paul worked as a team with men like Barnabas, Silas and Timothy. Silas and Barnabas worked together. The apostles in Jerusalem sent a team to Samaria and to Antioch when revival began in those areas. God's plan for the local church and for mission endeavors is never a one man show. The apostles, prophets, evangelists, teachers, pastors and laymen are to work together as teams.

When we operate as God has planned, we find protection from the enticements of Satan. Team ministry is a safeguard against sins which are common temptations when a person travels and ministers alone.

A Call to Youth

God always has His eyes on the younger generation. He has always used young people. Perhaps this is because they don't know what the traditional parameters are. If there is a big assignment to complete, they do it, and then ask questions.

Throughout the Bible when God had a big job to do, He often called a young person.

Young people have always been at the forefront of world missions. In this generation, God is reviving the hearts of young people to be a military force which will forcibly advance the kingdom of God.

All around the world a new generation of young people is fully committed to Jesus and to world evangelism. They refuse to tolerate half-hearted commitment in themselves and in others. Young people can heroically change the world.

SUMMARY

The church is facing the greatest challenge it has ever faced, to fulfill the Great Commission as this century is rapidly coming to its final hour. It's time to run to the battle - not from the battle.

The church is well able to fulfill the Great Commission. The church is well able to conquer the cities and nations where God sends us.

The church is equipped for the battle.

When Goliath came against David, Goliath insulted and tried to intimidate David.

The devil tries the same tactics today. He tries to intimidate us by causing us to look at our failures, pointing out that we are inept children and certainly no match for him.

David avoided this trap. He did not go up against Goliath in his own strength, but in the strength of God.

David could not be compared to the strength, power and skill of Goliath. But it took only one pebble to bring Goliath down with all of his great power.

As the body of Christ, the church must stop looking at its failure, weaknesses and defeats. It must begin to act in boldness.

In the thick of the conflict, we must not retreat. We must lift the banner, blow the trumpet and proclaim our victory! We are more than conquerors! We are triumphant in Christ Jesus!

David was aggressive with the knowledge he had. David was anointed to be king. We too are anointed. Our anointing is to preach the gospel to the lost. The church must be strong, bold and courageous because the weapons of our warfare are mighty through God to the pulling down of strongholds.

The spirit of boldness, the pioneer spirit, that was on Joshua is on the church. Wandering in the wilderness is over. It's time to possess our promised land. It's time to act in faith based on the word of God. Signs and wonders will follow us! Together, we will fulfill the Great Commission and take the gospel to every creature through miracle evangelism.

QUESTIONS FOR REVIEW

1. What is the primary purpose for the prosperity message?

2. What is meant by the "Pioneer Spirit of Evangelism"?

3. Give Biblical examples of team ministry for evangelism.